Mark

Tales
of the
Human Spirit
True Stories Well Told

8-16-22

Alan,

Hope you enjoy
the book, esp.
Pac man on p199!

Go Manny

Mark Fillman

651-352-8869

moina56@yahoo.com

**outskirts
press**

To Nelia, with love.

Table of Contents

POPULAR CULTURE/ ENTERTAINMENT

The Mysteries of
Inger Stevens

INGEBORG WAS A Norse princess with a star-crossed love life. Her name was the inspiration for Mr. and Mrs. Stensland to call their first-born daughter Inger. Inger Stensland grew up to be a beautiful star-crossed actress better known as Inger Stevens, whose dramatic death at a young age remains controversial even today.

Inger was best known for her role as Katy Holstrum in the 1960's television series *The Farmer's Daughter.* It was a breakout role for Inger, leading to more high-profile roles on screens large and small. Less well known was Inger's string of impetuous love affairs with her leading men. This may have led to her sudden death on April 30, 1970.

To understand her death it is best to start with her life, which began on October 18, 1934. Growing up in Stockholm, Sweden, Inger became attracted to acting after watching her father, Per Gustaf, perform the role of Ebenezer Scrooge in a local amateur production.

Inger was the oldest and only daughter born to Per and his wife Lisbet. Inger had two younger brothers, Carl, and Peter, each born two years apart. Unfortunately for the children, both parents deserted them. When Inger was four her mother abandoned the family for another man, returning only to take Peter with her, which upset the two remaining children even more.

Inger and Carl lost their father when he moved to the United States during during the Second World War in 1940. Inger and Carl were left with the family maid. Eventually they were taken in by their aunt, Karin Stensland Junker, who was also an actress. By 1944 Per Stensland had an American bride and a job as a university teacher in New York City. He arranged for ten-year-old Inger and eight-year-old Carl to take a freighter from Sweden to America.

The children, who knew no English, got off the boat in New Orleans. Their father was not there to greet them. Instead, the Salvation Army performed an act of mercy by taking the two frightened children to New York to reunite with their dad and to meet their stepmother.

Inger and Carl were thrown into the New York public school system. Inger proved her competence and inner drive by learning English quickly and so thoroughly that most moviegoers thought she was American born; she had not even a trace of a Swedish accent.

Despite her intelligence and willpower, Inger felt frightened and lost. "I fit nowhere," she recalled. "I was awkward, shy, clumsy, ugly with freckles and had no chance of winning a beauty contest." Just as Inger and Carl started feeling comfortable, Per got a better teaching position at Kansas State University. In 1948 the family moved to Manhattan, Kansas.

Feeling no love or support from her parents, fifteen-year-old Inger ran away from home. Hopping a bus to Kansas City, the girl who saw herself as ugly starred in burlesque shows for a tidy $60 a week. Per tracked his daughter down and dragged her back to Manhattan. Biding time for her next getaway, Inger participated in theater and glee club. She graduated high school in 1952, packed her bags and left town, eventually landing in New York City to pursue an acting career.

Contrary to her poor self-image, Inger was strikingly beautiful, with natural blonde hair and fine facial features. Her graceful, natural manner added to her appeal. She partnered with advertising agent Anthony Soglio, who Americanized Inger's last name from Stensland to Stevens, and got her in some TV commercials for detergents and cigarettes. Another break was being accepted into Lee Strasberg's Actor's Studio. Stevens joined a class that included Paul Newman, Marlon Brando, James Dean and Robert Redford.

Inger rolled the dice and married her agent in 1955. She and Tony Soglio had a successful business relationship, but their marriage was a disaster from the start. Tony was very jealous and possessive, and Inger was independent. They split up in January 1956. It was the beginning of a pattern for Inger: falling for men who were emotionally unavailable or abusive to her. When the relationships ended Inger felt like the abandoned little girl she once was. Then she would fall in love again.

The next time was with a man old enough to *be* her father: Bing Crosby. Twenty-two-year-old Inger won a supporting role in the 1957 MGM drama *Man on Fire*. Crosby, playing the male lead, was thirty years older than Stevens. The tabloids probably dramatized the situation by reporting that Stevens became suicidal when Crosby married another woman. Later Inger would become suicidal for real.

She got positive reviews for *Man on Fire*. Now under contract with Paramount, Stevens got another plum role in 1958's *Cry Terror!* Her performance as the wife of male lead James Mason won positive attention from critics. And she almost died. Stevens and several other cast members were overcome by carbon monoxide poisoning during filming. Inger was in an oxygen tent for two days. It was her second brush with dramatic illness in a year. While filming *Man on Fire* Stevens was rushed to the hospital with acute appendicitis.

Next came a wannabe epic, *The Buccaneer* (also 1958). Inger co-starred with heavyweights Yul Brynner and Charlton Heston. Despite the stars and the influence of Cecil B. DeMilles, the movie fell flat, ending the directing ambitions of actor Anthony Quinn. Quinn's other ambition, to bed Stevens, was more successful. After shooting was over Quinn returned to his wife, leaving Inger alone and depressed. Later she would remark, "When the cruise is finished the romance may linger, but the relationship seems to shift and change. You tell yourself you'll never fall in love that way again, but it happens…"(See Sources for citation)

It happened with another married man, Harry Belafonte, the male lead in MGM's *The World, the Flesh and the Devil*. Inger was the female lead. Nature ran its course, the two had a passionate romance, the movie ended, and Belafonte returned to his marriage. On New Year's Day, 1959, Inger overdosed on pills and would have died but for the intervention of a friend who worried when Inger missed a social engagement and couldn't be reached by phone. Later Inger called her suicide attempt "stupid" and said she would never do it again.

The 1960's were Inger Steven's most visible years as an actress and TV personality. She rebounded from unhappy affairs and a suicide attempt by refocusing on her craft and staying busy. She was always in the public eye either through movies, theatrical productions, commercials, or television series.

In 1961, however, Stevens had another brush with death. She was vacationing in Europe when a plane she was in bounced off the runway in Lisbon. This started a fire that spread to the passenger cabin. Stevens was one of the last passengers off the plane, which then exploded. In her short life Inger had her full share of near-death experiences.

Speaking of death, Stevens starred in one of the most famous *Twilight Zone* episodes, "The Hitchhiker." She played Nan Adams, a young woman trying to cheat death, as personified by the hitchhiker stalking her throughout the episode. It is a chilling story. Stevens portrays her character's gradual awareness of her fate in a nuanced, gripping, and finally shattering performance.

In 1962 Stevens played opposite Peter Falk in a standalone episode called "The Price of Tomatoes," which aired on The Dick Powell Show. Inger was a pregnant Romanian girl evading immigration police, and Falk was the truck driver who befriended her. The show was so well-done Stevens and Falk were both nominated for Emmy awards.

The television show Stevens is most remembered for was *The Farmer's Daughter*, a network situation comedy that aired from 1963 to 1966. Stevens had to relearn her Swedish accent to play the role of Katy Holstrum, governess to Glen Morley, a widowed politician played by William Windom - one of the few leading men Stevens did not have an affair with. Windom later described Stevens as "a woman with many secrets." Only after her death would the truth of that statement fully penetrate.

The show was popular. Stevens won a Golden Globe Award, and the show garnered record ratings when Glen Morley and Katy Holstrum married at the beginning of the third season. Most viewers seemed to consider the story over after the honeymoon, for they tuned out. *The Farmer's Daughter* was canceled after its third season.

Inger was almost abnormally busy in the following

years. She appeared as Walter Mathau's wife (no affair there) in the 1967 comedy *A Guide For the Married Man.* Here Stevens had several semi-nude scenes, and an opportunity to demonstrate how physically fit her body was. She was very conscious of her physical appearance, and serious about dieting and exercising.

Then there was *Hang 'Em High* with Clint Eastwood, *5 Card Stud* with Dean Martin (affair) and Robert Mitchum, and *Madigan* with Henry Fonda and Richard Widmark. All three movies were done in 1968. The next two years were busy as well.

Stevens' last movie was the made for TV *Run Simon Run.* Inger starred with Burt Reynolds, a Native American seeking revenge for his brother's murder. Stevens played a social worker who eventually fell for Reynolds and helped him find the bad guys. Off screen she fell for Reynolds too.

In 1970 Inger Stevens had fifteen major movies to her credit, and just as many television and theatrical roles. She was delighted to be selected by Aaron Spelling to co-star in a new TV series, *The Most Deadly Game*, due to premiere in the fall. Stevens was cast as a criminologist solving unusual murders. The series was due to start filming in one short month. Inger seemed busy, happy, and successful.

At approximately 7:30 pm Wednesday evening, April 29, 1970, Burt Reynolds left Inger Stevens' house after having an argument with her. At 11 pm Stevens called her personal assistant, Chris Bone, and said she had argued with Burt, and had drank two glasses of wine. Stevens told Chris she was going to take a sleeping pill and go to bed.

The next morning a friend came by Inger's house and found her lying face down on the kitchen floor. She was dressed in a nightgown and a scruffy pair of slippers. The friend said Inger opened her eyes, tried to speak, and fell unconscious. There was a cut on her chin covered by a band-aid, and an abrasion on her arm. An ambulance took Stevens to Hollywood Receiving Hospital. She was pronounced dead on arrival at 10:30 am.

At 1:30 pm an autopsy was performed at the County Coroner's office. Her blood alcohol content was 0.17. It was estimated there were 25-50 barbiturate pills in Steven's stomach. The cause of death was labeled "acute barbiturate intoxication due to ingestion of overdose."

Surprises continued when a man named Ike Jones stepped forward to claim the body, saying he was Inger Steven's husband. Inger's brother Carl and her father and stepmother came into town. The group had a private memorial service on May 4. The next day Inger's body was cremated, and the ashes scattered into the Pacific Ocean.

Turns out Inger and Ike married in Tijuana, Mexico on November 18, 1961. Jones was an athlete at UCLA and had a versatile career as a musician, actor, and movie producer. The two kept their marriage a secret for fear it would damage Steven's career. Marriages between black men and white women were not popular in the 1960's, as evidenced by actress Mai Britt's career plunge when she married Sammy Davis Junior.

Jones' claim to be Steven's husband was challenged in court. Inger's brother Carl supported Jones' claims, and although there was considerable conflicting evidence on the matter, Jones was eventually awarded Inger Steven's estate. He said that after all the bills got paid there was nothing left over - kind of like their marriage. It seems Ike's relationship with Inger was like her relationships with other men: often strained, with long periods of separation. It does not seem that either husband or wife took their vows of fidelity seriously. At the time of her death the two were estranged.

For most, that is the end of the story. How could there

be any other conclusion than that Inger Stevens finally completed a suicide attempt? She had already attempted suicide once. Her strained relationship with Burt Reynolds was perhaps the final straw.

But to some that answer is not so easy. Steven's family and close friends are unanimous in their belief that Inger did not commit suicide. They point out that up until the morning of April 30, 1970, Stevens gave every impression of being happy with her life. She was focusing on short term and long-term plans for her career. She was getting roles she liked and was staying in the public eye. True, she was having relationship problems, but that was nothing new, and besides, she had sworn off suicide as a remedy.

Inger's personal assistant, Chris Bone, does not believe Stevens killed herself either. She believes that if Inger was really going to kill herself, she would have worn makeup and dressed properly. Stevens herself said she had learned enough from her first suicide attempt to never go down that road again.

William Patterson is a private investigator who wrote a book about Inger Stevens. He also doubts the official verdict. He examined the physical evidence in the room, noting a bottle of pills that did not belong to Stevens. The cut on the chin and abrasion on the arm indicate someone had been physically violent with Inger. She also had an IUD in place, which Patterson thought was significant. From the physical evidence in the room, it seemed that Stevens had been in the middle of making her favorite sandwich when she died.

Patterson notes there were asthma pills containing Phenobarbital (a barbiturate) laying on the living room floor. They came from a small pill bottle labeled Tedral that did not contain doctor or pharmacy information. The bottle probably did not belong to Stevens, as she did not have asthma. There were also Seconal tablets scattered on the bedroom floor. Inger typically did not take sedatives to get to sleep. Patterson has a murder suspect who he does not name for legal reasons. His theory is that someone who knew Inger visited her but then forced her to swallow enough pills to kill herself. The motive is unclear, but it can be assumed to be personal.

This conclusion may be too lurid for some. The other theory, that maybe Inger took a few more pills than prescribed after she had the fight with Reynolds, and accidentally overdosed, doesn't hold up. Twenty-five to fifty pills is not just "a few more". That quantity of pills is only ingested with suicidal intent. But to commit suicide at such an exciting part of her life, and when she was so involved and enthusiastic with her projects, well, that doesn't make sense either.

What we do know is a young life ended too early. Inger had many friends, admirers, and fans who were left heartbroken. For all her successes in her chosen field, Inger was often heartbroken too. And she spoke frankly about life in Hollywood: "A career can't put its arms around you. You end up like Grand Central Station with people just coming and going. And there you are, left alone."

In a chapter dedicated to her in Kirk Crivello's book *Fallen Angels*, Inger said:

"Once I felt that I was one person at home and the minute I stepped out the door I had to be somebody else. I had a terrific insecurity and extreme shyness that I covered up with coldness. Everybody thought I was a snob. I was really just plain scared."

Hollywood columnist Ben Irwin's eulogy: "[She was] essentially a hopeful and gay human being capable of imparting that to others . . . For that really was what Inger was about—honesty and love. And she spent her life working harder than most of us practicing the first and living the second."

Jerry Lem, the primary contributor to her online memorial website, adds: "Inger remains a gifted actress, an unforgettably beautiful woman and a kind, caring human being who lives on in our memories. The years since her untimely death have done little to diminish the impression she left us—Her legacy has touched our lives."

Inger Stensland, *Requiescat in pacem.*

Sources

Inger Stevens: Wounded Butterfly, by Gary Brumburgh. This is the source for the quote by Inger that began "I fit in nowhere."

http://www.classicimages.com/people/article_1e7f82c6-bac3-57e9-a1bb-2d301aee1af7.html

http://www.ingerstevens.org/, a memorial website run by Jerry Lem, with much interesting information on the life of Inger Stevens. I am indebted to Jerry for critiquing this article and providing me with a wealth of detail surrounding Inger and her last days. This is the source for the eulogy remarks.

Kirk Crivello, *Fallen Angels: The Lives And Untimely Deaths Of 14 Hollywood Beauties*, Warner Paperbacks, 1988. Source for "Once I felt..."

William Patterson, *The Farmer's Daughter Remembered: The Biography of Actress Inger Stevens* (Foreword by William Windom), published 2000. This is the source for Inger's quote: "When the cruise is finished..."

A Hallelujah for Leonard Cohen

LEONARD COHEN IS so quiet and self-contained that in talking with him you would never realize he has won awards for his poetry, writing and singing in five consecutive decades. What you might notice instead are pervasive clouds of heavy seriousness he disperses with witty quips - quips which are also used to deflect the topic of conversation when the topic is why Cohen is called the "high priest of pathos."

That is not Cohen's only nickname. After all, in six decades of performing he was bound to pick up a few monikers. Like this one: "The poet laureate of pessimism." Or this: "The prince of bummers." Or: "grocer of despair." Or: "Godfather of gloom." Or...well, you get the point.

Kurt Cobain wrote about longing for a 'Leonard Cohen afterworld where I could sigh eternally'. His tunes have been referred to as "music to slit your wrists by." At times Cohen has gone along with the joke, once suggesting his record company give away razor blades with his records.

The Grim Reaper of Words and Moods does not live up to his reputation when you meet him in person. Instead of a dark cloaked and hooded figure, Cohen in person displays a clever, utterly self-mocking sense of humor that doesn't always show up on a lyric sheet.

He has always been a writer. He started getting published in 1956. By the time he picked up songwriting and guitar playing he had already published several novels and poetry books. Cohen began releasing records in the 1960's and he hasn't stopped, although he has gone on hiatus from time to time. But before his first song was ever recorded, nine-year-old Leonard Cohen wrote a poem for his dead father that he wrapped around his father's favorite bow tie and buried in the ground.

Writing is in Cohen's bones, deeply ancestral, tracing perhaps all the way back to the venerable "priesthood of Aaron," which Cohen's (formerly Kohen) parents solemnly informed little Leonard was his lineage.

What is a child to make of *that* moniker? To round off Cohen's Polish-Lithuanian Jewish ancestry, his maternal grandfather, Rabbi Solomon Kline, wrote a 700-page thesaurus of Talmudic interpretations. Evidently the Rabbi passed on his gift for writing to his grandson.

The Talmud and the priesthood of Aaron were not commonplace notions in the middle-class Protestant suburb of Montreal Leonard Cohen grew up in. Montreal in the 1930's was overwhelmingly Catholic, Protestant, and white. Yet a noticeable minority of Jews co-existed with the majorities, politely (or otherwise) ignoring cathedrals, statues of saints and street names, while giving and receiving sustenance in small private enclaves.

The adult Leonard Cohen looks back and recalls, "I had a very Messianic childhood." It was a beginning that would inform his art again and again. Even today, at age eighty, Cohen reflects: "I grew up in a very conservative, observant family...It's not something I have to publicize or display, but it is essential to my own survival. Those are values that my family gave me, which are Torah values...I never stray very far from those influences."

Cohen attended public schools, where his interests in poetry and music were evident early on. In the Westmount High School yearbook Cohen is quoted as wishing to become a "world famous orator." He also became enamored of Spanish poet Federico Garcia Lorca.

Lorca was a Spanish socialist, writer, and playwright assassinated during the Spanish Civil War. Although his physical body was never found, Lorca's body of work has attracted an avant-garde following which includes Leonard Cohen, who named his daughter Lorca.

At McGill University Cohen majored in literature and poetry, and created his first band, the Buckskin Boys. Cohen and two friends wore buckskin with phony ponytails and played for square dances in church halls. It was a completely underwhelming start to a notable and well-studied musical career. After the Buckskin Boys went the way of the dodo bird, Cohen published his first book, which he dedicated to his father. *Let Us Compare Mythologies* was a series of poems published in 1956.

At that point Cohen had graduated college and was trying to make a career for himself as a poet, writer, and general literary genius. He had two novels and several poetry books published. Overall, his work was critically praised and occasionally controversial. For instance, Cohen's second novel, *Beautiful Losers,* in the eyes of one reviewer was "the most revolting book ever written in Canada". Ouch.

The main problem, however, was that no one outside of Leonard's small literary circle of literary friends bought any of his books. "It was very difficult to pay my grocery bill," Cohen said later. "I've got beautiful reviews for all my books, and I'm very well thought of in the tiny circles that know me, but...I'm really starving."

Hunger pangs led Cohen to songwriting. It was not a

difficult switch because Cohen was still using words, which are his medium:

> "I always feel that the world was created through words, through speech in our tradition, and I've always seen the enormous light in charged speech. "That's what I've tried to get to [and] that is where I squarely stand."

Sometimes Cohen entered his stance through muses. The first was Marianne Ihlen, his lover in the early 1960's. The two lived on the Greek island of Hydra. It was there Cohen began developing his body of work, which eventually included a song for his muse: (So Long) Marianne.

Cohen's next muse, Suzanne, also got a song named after her, and two children (Adam and Lorca) with Leonard as well. Other influences on Cohen were Zen Catholic novelist Jack Kerouac, and country singer Hank Williams. Williams was such a strong influence that in 1966 Cohen, back in Canada by now, determined to travel to Nashville to do a country album. On the way he stopped in Greenwich Village and had fateful meetings with folk artists Bob Dylan, Joan Baez, Judy Collins, Joni Mitchell, and others. He didn't make it to Nashville - that time.

Cohen was older than his new friends. He was already in his thirties, a published writer, and was in several respects farther along the literary and artistic track than Dylan and the others. Many of them looked up to the older Cohen. Judy Collins recorded Cohen's signature song "Suzanne" before he did.

Collins' sponsorship of Cohen caught the eye of Columbia Records. Cohen recorded three albums for Columbia: *Songs of Leonard Cohen, Songs from a Room,* and *Songs of Love and Hate.* His early work was similar to his folkie friends, but not imitative. Cohen was more mature and restrained than his contemporaries, who often got swept away musically with passing social and political situations. Lyrically he was remarkably lean and concise, but also imaginary and evocative. His words could be interpreted in layers, but the lyrics were also accessible. His musical arrangements were very spare. Whether words or notes, Cohen pared everything to the bone.

Early on Cohen figured out how to assimilate his poetic talents into the singer-songwriter format of folk music without insulting his muses or failing the requirements of his new medium. His lyrics are a remarkable combination of poetry, fiction, autobiography, religion, politics, and sexuality. For the next several decades Leonard Cohen released albums in a leisurely, sometimes sporadic, fashion.

In 1984 Cohen created perhaps his most famous song: Hallelujah. It is a song that has been covered literally dozens of times by artists all over the world. In some circles it is as well-known as "Jingle Bells." Hallelujah originally appeared on Cohen's 1984 release "Various Positions." He reportedly wrote and rewrote the song dozens of times before he was satisfied with the result.

Hallelujah begins as an Old Testament morality play and turns into a story about the human search for transcendence - spiritual and sexual yearnings for *more* that either don't happen or don't last. Yet even the failed attempts at transcendence can evoke "a cold and a broken Hallelujah," for the realization that at least our human condition gives us the chance to reach for and even have transcendence for a moment, albeit with the certainty of a future of renewed longings when the transcendence, like all things, passes away.

The lyrics are "rapturously bleak," and Cohen's vocal delivery in the original is dispassionate. Yet the mood of the song can be joyous, bittersweet. or both. Everyone else who has covered Hallelujah has been closer to the joyous, even histrionic end of the scale. In 2008 a poll of 50 songwriters ranked Hallelujah as one of the ten best songs of all time. *Rolling Stone* also had Hallelujah as a "best of." The song inspired a BBC documentary and at least one book.

When Cohen talked with Bob Dylan about his writing process on Hallelujah, Dylan told Cohen every song he wrote was done in a few minutes. Not so with Cohen. He took the long way round to songwriting. This is one of the reasons his album releases were so occasional. Cohen never went into the studio with the goal of banging out an album in a certain time frame. He was always the poet and the artist, serious to the point of obsession about his craft, taking as much time as it took to hone the lyrics and music down to its essence.

Cohen never settled for lightweight songs. He went for the jugular every time. Sometimes he succeeded and sometimes he missed. But you had the sense that he was always down there digging for something. Writer Pico Iyer wrote of Cohen:

> "The changeless is what he's been about since the beginning...Some of the other great pilgrims of song pass through philosophies and selves as if through the stations of the cross. With Cohen, one feels he knew who he was and where he was going from the beginning, and only digs deeper, deeper, deeper."

In the 1990's Cohen dug for Zen. "It was one of the many attempts I've made in the past 30 or 40 years to address acute clinical depression," he declared. As for other remedies (drugs), Cohen remarked: "The recreational, the obsessional and the pharmaceutical - I've tried them all.

I would be enthusiastically promoting any one of them if they worked."

Buddhism sounded like Cohen's last resort. It is not known if he uttered a Hallelujah upon disappearing into the sparse quarters of Mount Baldy Monastery in southern California. It is known that he emerged from the monastery an ordained Zen Buddhist monk, after spending five consecutive years living life without distractions under the watchful eye of Zen master Joshu Sasaki-Roshi.

In 2001, at the age of sixty-seven, Leonard Cohen released an album called *Ten New Songs*. It was a hit in Europe, and in Cohen's own Canada. There followed a series of albums and world tours, all of which were well received. In 2008 Cohen was inducted into the Rock and Roll Hall of Fame. He received a Grammy Award for lifetime achievement in 2010.

Canada has not forgotten its own son either. Leonard Cohen has been inducted into the Canadian Music Hall of Fame and the Canadian Songwriters Hall of Fame. In 2011 Cohen was given a Princess of Asturias Award. He has also been made a Companion of the Order of Canada, which is Canada's highest civilian honor.

With accolades came agony. Cohen discovered his life savings of five million dollars was stolen by his former manager and friend. He has been unable to recoup his losses. So, part of Cohen's motivation to keep playing and releasing albums is financial: he needs the money. Fortunately, he seems to have discovered a remarkable new musical plateau; or perhaps in Cohen's case it is more accurate to say that he has plumbed downward to discover an underground spring of living water.

In 2012 Cohen released Old Ideas, which became the highest charting album in his entire career. Then in 2014, at the age of eighty, Cohen released Popular Problems, his thirteenth album. Again, it was warmly received. In 2016 another album appeared: You Want It Darker. In an interview with the *New Yorker*, Cohen declared: "I am ready to die. I hope it's not too uncomfortable. That's about it for me."

Many of Cohen's friends and fans were not ready for Cohen to pass behind the curtain. Cohen addressed the uproar in his usual fashion: he threw cold water on himself. "I've always been into self-dramatization," he reassured everyone. "I intend to live forever."

On November 7 2016 Leonard Cohen died after falling in his home in Los Angeles. He was 82 years old. He left two children, Adam and Lorca, and several grandchildren. Adam released a brief statement that his father had passed away peacefully in the knowledge that his last recording was "one of his greatest records."

Cohen's body was taken back to his hometown of Montreal for burial. His passing created an outpouring of grief and acclaim for his career and his singular talent. Here is some of that praise.

Nick Cave: "For many of us Leonard Cohen was the greatest songwriter of them all. Utterly unique and impossible to imitate no matter how hard we tried. He will be deeply missed by so many."

Robert Cory, Cohen's producer: "Unmatched in his creativity, insight and crippling candour, Leonard Cohen was a true visionary whose voice will be sorely missed. I was blessed to call him a friend, and for me to serve that bold artistic spirit firsthand was a privilege and great gift. He leaves behind a legacy of work that will bring insight, inspiration and healing for generations to come."

Sylvie Simmons, Cohen's biographer: "He went out in

a blaze of glory. Died with his boots on – or his suit on – having delivered a masterpiece before he left. You Want it Darker is one of his richest, deepest and most beautiful albums in a lifetime of rich, deep and beautiful work. So many stories about musicians and poets have an unhappy ending but not Leonard."

John Cale: "Very upsetting news to learn of Leonard's passing. The world has one less gentle soul tonight. We thank you for the multitude of gifts you left us."

Beck: "So long Leonard, thank you for your words, your songs, your life – a gentleman, a master, a hero – thank you for looking so deeply, for sharing your time, giving us your finely wrought diamonds, for lighting the dark corners where the soul lives, for translating the otherness we recognize but fail to express, tonight we celebrate you and send you our gratitude."

Cat Stevens: "The fragileness of life has been once again exposed with the passing on of Leonard Cohen. May God grant him peace … forever."

Russell Crowe: "Dear Leonard Cohen, thanks for the quiet nights, the reflection, the perspective, the wry smiles and the truth."

Boy George: "We have lost a great artist, poet and poignant force of energy. R.I.P Leonard Cohen."

Elton John called Cohen "unique – a giant of a man and a brilliant songwriter. Irreplaceable. Loved him and his wonderful music."

And finally, the man Leonard Cohen influenced perhaps most of all: Bob Dylan, whose most famous quote on Cohen was "He doesn't write songs, he writes prayers." Dylan said:

"When people talk about Leonard, they fail to mention his melodies, which to me, along with his lyrics, are his greatest genius. Even the counterpoint lines—they give a celestial character and melodic lift to every one of his songs. As far as I know, no one else comes close to this in modern music."

Leonard Cohen, *Requiescat in pacem*

SOURCES

http://www.leonardcohen.com/

http://www.leonardcohenfiles.com/

http://www.newyorker.com/culture/culture-desk/leonard-cohens-montreal

http://www.theguardian.com/theobserver/2001/oct/14/features.magazine37

https://rockhall.com/inductees/leonard-cohen/bio/

http://www.rollingstone.com/music/artists/leonard-cohen/biography

uk guardian http://www.uncut.co.uk/features/leonard-cohen

http://www.theguardian.com/music/2014/sep/21/leonard-cohen-life-as-an-outsider-80th-birthday

The quotes at the end of the article are all from the US version of *The Guardian,* in an obituary penned by Hannah Ellis-Petersen in its November 11 2016 issue. See https://www.theguardian.com/music/2016/nov/11/stars-musicians-world-leaders-pay-tribute-leonard-cohen.

The Amazing Afterlife of Eva Cassidy

ONCE THERE WAS a golden voice aimed like an arrow to the hearts of all who heard it. The voice belonged to Eva Cassidy: a songbird whose life ended too soon, but whose music has grown in popularity despite her untimely death.

She was a blue-eyed, blond-haired Aquarian of Scotch, Irish, and German descent. Eva's dad Hugh was a musician who played bass and cello. He gave nine-year-old Eva a guitar and taught her some chords. Eva's little brother Daniel joined in, and Eva's two older sisters as well. With Hugh as maestro, the family entertained relatives and friends at social gatherings.

Eva's teenage musical tastes were varied: Stevie Wonder, Joan Baez, Ella Fitzgerald, and Pete Seeger to name a few. She taught herself guitar, and then piano. While her musical gifts were obvious, Eva struggled singing publicly due to extreme shyness. She persevered, playing with local bands, and at a theme park near her birthplace of Washington D.C. But music was a hobby at this point. Eva dabbled in community college as well, but to make ends meet she worked in a plant nursery and as a furniture painter with a penchant for pastels.

Cassidy's boyfriend, Chris Blondo, found Eva a string of

musical projects singing backup vocals and sitting in as a session singer for a variety of musical acts. This led to Blondo and Cassidy forming the "Eva Cassidy Band" in 1990. Blondo, who was one of Eva's first fans, played a tape of her songs for Chuck Brown, a legendary musician in the D.C. area. Brown was not easy to please, but when he heard Eva's voice he flipped.

Mr. Brown was a convicted murderer who learned guitar in prison. He did his time and reformed his life. Brown is credited for forming a sub-genre of black funk known as "go-go." The "Godfather of go-go" and the shy, Irish Catholic Eva Cassidy were an odd couple visually, but musically they clicked.

In 1992 the two collaborated on *The Other Side*, an album of blues and jazz standards released on Brown's label, Liaison Records. The most enduring song from the album was Cassidy's solo cover of "Somewhere Over the Rainbow." It is hard to believe anyone could top Judy Garland's version, but Eva's cover was an absolute tour de force and very popular today.

After the album with Brown, Eva had more opportunities to perform. While she loved music, she was still shy playing and singing in public. She was more at ease painting, hiking or biking, or driving out of D.C. and into nature - often with her mother Barbara.

Barbara recalled Eva driving a beat up old pick-up truck out to the country and swerving all over the road. An alarmed mom questioned her behavior. Eva replied, "Mom, don't you see the caterpillars? I can't run them over."

It was behavior worthy of a Buddhist monk, but Eva wasn't churchgoing. Her friend and band mate Keith Grimes remembers: "She's one of those people who see God in everything. She had respect and appreciation for living things...she was spiritual."

Perhaps it was this quiet spiritual aspect to Cassidy that

made her voice and her music so compelling. In 1993 she performed "Over the Rainbow" at the Washington Area Music Association. A Washington Times review called her rendition a "showstopper." Cassidy received a "Wammie" award in the best Vocalist Jazz/Traditional category.

But Eva's refusal to be slotted into a particular singing genre (folk, jazz, blues) kept her commercially obscure. Unable to land a record deal, Cassidy and Blondo released a live album of Eva's performances at *Blues Alley* in Washington D.C. Eva had a cold when performing and was disappointed with the results. She did not want to release the album. Eventually "Live at Blues Alley" came out and received critical praise. A *Washington Post* reviewer said of Eva: "She could sing anything — folk, blues, pop, jazz, R&B, gospel — and make it sound like it was the only music that mattered."

As the album was released Eva discovered she had cancer in her lungs and bones. Aggressive chemotherapy was not enough to stop the spread of the disease. Eva's final live performance was at a benefit concert for herself. The last song she sang in public was "What a Wonderful World." The audience, consisting of fans, friends, and family, must have felt the poignant ache of those words.

The benefit raised $10,000. Eva gave the money to some young cancer patients she had met earlier in the hospital and wrote over 100 thank you notes to people who attended her benefit.

Eva died at her parent's home in Bowie Maryland on November 2, 1996. She was thirty-three years old. Her body was cremated and, as she wished, her ashes were scattered in St. Mary's River Watershed Park, a nature reserve she loved to visit.

Two years later Eva's family compiled some of her music into an album called *Songbird*. Like Eva's other records, it remained obscure. She was unknown outside of Washington

D.C. until, way across the ocean, English deejay Terry Wogan played a couple of Eva's songs on his BBC Radio show.

The British audience fell in love with Eva's renditions of "Over the Rainbow" and Sting's "Fields of Gold." Critics and fans raved about her soprano voice, her singing range, and her perfect phrasing. It sounded like Eva's heart was singing the songs, and people responded. Eva's English fans included Sir Paul McCartney and Eric Clapton. *Songbird* topped the charts in England before 2000.

More albums from Eva came out posthumously, as well as a biography in 2001 titled *Songbird: Eva Cassidy: Her Story by Those Who Knew Her.* The book has sold well enough to have an American edition containing extra material. Her life has also been portrayed in a musical. There is even talk of a movie.

American figure skater Michelle Kwan skated to "Fields of Gold" while performing in the 2002 Winter Olympics figure skating competition. Eva's recording of "Autumn Leaves" was performed too by Andre and Natalie Paramonov during the finals of the International Latin Ballroom Competition.

The album *A Tribute to Eva Cassidy* was released in 2012, the same year that another biography of Eva, *Behind the Rainbow* by Johan Bakker, won The People's Book Prize.

After *Songbird*, four CDs of Eva's music have been released posthumously. *Time After Time* in 2000, *Imagine* in 2002, *American Tune* in 2003, *Somewhere* in 2008, and *Simply Eva* in 2011.

The tributes and appreciation for the musical talents of Eva Cassidy is gratifying to her family and friends. They wish Eva was still alive to appreciate the adulation. Eva, however, never really cared for fame. She wanted to touch people's hearts, and then go on her way. And so she has.

Eva Marie Cassidy, *requiescat in pacem.*

Heroes: David Bowie and Family

WE ENDOW OUR cultural legends with abilities so mythic they can seem immune to travails of life like illness, dying and death. David Bowie is such a legend, even if he now must be referred to in the past tense.

That is how *Time* referred to him in their commemorative magazine edition titled: *David Bowie: His Life on Earth*. Fully illustrated too. Pretty legendary send off for Mister Bowie, isn't it? How many of us will have our fully illustrated careers commemorated in a special edition of *Time* magazine?

Yet we minions do have something in common with legends like David Bowie. We all die. Bowie was a singular artist, a larger-than-life cultural presence for decades. And he still ended up on a slab. We all will. Inevitably the body gives up the ghost: that animating force, the spirit, the spark, the flame, that precious essence of our humanity – Poof! Gone, gone away to Never land.

Bowie and his family were intensely private. Only in death does the curtain lift to reveal Bowie battled liver cancer for 18 months; a fact he kept from even his best friends - now that's *private*.

The curtain raises higher, and we discover how Bowie

fought cancer by defiantly living a normal life. He kept his hopes and dreams alive by focusing on his art. For projects that extended into the future, Bowie disclosed his diagnosis when professionally necessary – to warn collaborators of the rude speed bump ahead.

Bowie was loved by a wife, son, and daughter. They helped him, laughed, joked, and cried with him, and held him at his bedside as he died. It is all so normal sounding it reminds us of deaths in our own families.

An old girlfriend introduced me to David Bowie. I liked some of his singles, but his fashion sense left me cold as an outdoor hockey rink. I finally listened to one of his albums straight through: *Young Americans.* I was surprised how good it was. Although I was (and am) selective with Bowie's catalog, I liked how he stuck the boot in on songs like "The Gene Genie", "Suffragette City," "Rebel Rebel," and of course, "Heroes," the epic Berlin Wall love story. And I warmed to his eccentricities: songs like "China Girl" and especially "Breaking Glass," a hilarious oddity. It was also funny when my girlfriend became my wife and we both liked Bowie. It got unfunny when our marriage died, and she became (among other things) my ex-wife. Death doesn't always have a sense of humor, but you have to admit: it is *very* reliable.

Bowie had an ex-wife too, Her name was Angela. She married David when she was twenty. They made headlines as the world's first openly bisexual celebrity couple. Behind the glam fashions, Angela says the two struck a deal: she would help David launch his career, then he would do the same for her theatrical career. According to Angela, she not only kept up her side of the bargain, she also helped her hubby create and market his Ziggy Stardust persona.

Then fame (*Fame, Fame, Fame, Fame, Fame, what's your name what's your name...*) came calling and the two drifted apart. David and Angela's marriage was ship-wrecked by sex and drugs but saved – for a time - by rock and roll. After ten years the marriage died and was given a public autopsy.

A court in Switzerland gave Bowie full custody of the couple's only child, whose legal name is Zowie (probably doesn't rhyme with Bowie). Dad getting the kid(s) is always a sign mom is a train wreck - which, unfortunately, Angela was at this point in her life.

When the divorce "gag order" expired Angela penned the obligatory bitter autobiography (*"come read the juicy details about what a psychopathic sexual deviant horror show my ex-husband was"*). Angela said David "had the instincts of a bisexual alley cat," accused him of having an affair with Mick Jagger while still married to her, and of turning their son Zowie against her. David contented himself with remarking that his marriage to Angie was "like living with a blow torch." (See Sources for citation)

Zowie, meanwhile, grew into a seemingly sensible 44-year-old filmmaker who today calls himself Duncan Jones. Surely Dad could take some credit for that.

Unlike his mom, Duncan is on good terms with the legend. The morning of January 11 Duncan posted an old picture of his dad holding him, with the words: "Very sorry and sad to say that it is true..." Daddy's death left a big hole in the Bowie family: a hole giving outsiders access to their supremely private lives.

After Angela, David was married to his second wife, Iman, for nearly 25 years. She and their daughter Lexie were also at his bedside, though not for the first time. For in 2004 David had a heart attack from a clogged artery. It is said Iman nursed him back to health and raised Lexie too, who was four. Mrs. Bowie is also larger than life: a supermodel, one of the most gorgeous women on the planet.

How did she become enamored of a skinny, eccentric Brit like David Bowie?

The two superstars met on a blind date. Bowie declared his attraction to Iman "was immediate and all-encompassing." Sure, him and a million other guys.

"That she would be my wife, in my head, was a done deal," he said. "I'd never gone after anything in my life with such passion in all my life. I just knew she was the one."

He was right. And along with her fabulous appeal, Iman was a good wife and mother. In 2000 she and David had a daughter: Alexandria Zahra Jones, known as "Lexie." Anyone wonder what the Bowie parenting roles were? According to Iman: "David is measured, sensible yet at the same time fun and relaxed with Lexi. I'm the disciplinarian!"

Sounds like Ziggy Stardust was a good dad. While the Bowie's had homes in London and Mustique, their home base was New York. They managed a jet-set lifestyle (his music, her beauty career) and had an intact family world very few people knew about. Iman said: "I am married to David Jones. David Bowie and David Jones are two totally different people."

Some would say Bowie is ten or twelve different people. But to keep things relatively simple, Bowie was first David Jones, a young artist concerned about being confused with (or overshadowed by) Davey Jones of Monkees fame. Indeed, Davey shot to mega stardom, leaving David Jones to a series of musical flops.

But little David Jones had Big Imagination, fueled and informed by American movies and music. David's father gave him 45 rpms from artists like Elvis Presley and Little Richard, whose light it up tune "Tutti Frutti" caused Bowie to say later: "I had heard God". Presley's "Hound Dog" had a similar impact. Bowie saw the visceral reaction of the audiences, and the power they gave over to the artist to influence their emotions and their bodies.

The cinema was equally powerful. David Jones, the lonely white kid from a London suburb, decided he was going to change his name to David Bowie in honor of the American Jim Bowie who died during the siege of the Alamo (at least as Bowie was portrayed by Richard Widmark in the American movie "The Alamo").

Never mind that Bowie didn't play with knives or give his life for a cause. The name change merged Bowie's infatuation with American music and American movies. Funny thing is the name change seemed to ch-ch-ch-ch-change everything.

In retrospect the Bowie persona became a platform for him to experiment with characters and outrageous fashions; to present rock and roll as a cinematic event, a movie even; but with accompanying music that was at times brilliant, and often very good.

So began the career of David Bowie, which Rolling Stone aptly described:

"Ever unpredictable, the mercurial artist and fashion icon wore many guises throughout his life. Beginning life as a dissident folk-rock spaceman, he would become an androgynous, orange-haired, glam-rock alien (Ziggy Stardust), a well-dressed, blue-eyed funk maestro (the Thin White Duke), a drug-loving art rocker (the Berlin albums), a new-wave hit-maker, a hard rocker, a techno enthusiast and a jazz impressionist. His flair for theatricality won him a legion of fans." (See Sources for citation).

For decades most of Bowie's fans stuck with *him* - not the various personas he developed (with the possible exception of Ziggy Stardust). It was a gig that went on for five decades, influencing countless artists from Nirvana to Kanye West.

The singer kept his cancer diagnosis secret, even to some of his closest friends. But the director of Bowie's off-Broadway play Lazarus, Ivo van Hove, said Bowie told him right away that he was battling liver cancer and would miss some rehearsals. In a radio interview van Hove remarked:

"Bowie was still writing on his deathbed... I saw a man fighting. He fought like a lion and kept working like a lion through it all. I had incredible respect for that."

On Friday, two days before his death, Iman helped her husband celebrate his 69th birthday and the release of his new album, "Blackstar." That is right: Bowie's last album, released posthumously, is called "Blackstar." You can't make it up.

Bowie did not intend Blackstar to be his last album. It is in no way a summation of his career. The legend thought he had one more album in him. His longtime producer, Tony Visconti, remarked:

"He always did what he wanted to do, and he wanted to do it his way and he wanted to do it the best way. His death was no different from his life – a work of art. He made Blackstar for us, his parting gift. I knew for a year this was the way it would be. I wasn't, however, prepared for it. He was an extraordinary man, full of love and life. He will always be with us. For now, it is appropriate to cry." (See Sources for citation)

Which is what many fans did when Bowie's Facebook page released this announcement: "David Bowie died peacefully today surrounded by his family after a courageous 18-month battle with cancer. While many of you will share in this loss, we ask that you respect the family's privacy during their time of grief." (See Sources for citation)

If fans and friends couldn't get past the Bowie family picket fence, they could settle for buying his last album and going to the last off-Broadway show Bowie was involved with, *Lazarus*. Perhaps the covert hope that Bowie might resurrect himself like Lazarus and appear on stage just one more time fueled the outrageously priced ticket sales ($1,000 apiece). Some scalpers sold tickets for over $3,000, which proves that the bigger you are, the more bucks can be made off you.

Profits are no use to David Bowie now. Wherever he is, though, perhaps the love and appreciation of the millions for his art can somehow be absorbed by David Jones, Ziggy Stardust, The White Duke, the rock and roll legend, our friendly neighborhood super nova Lazarus.

The last words go to his biggest fan: Iman Bowie, who said that up until his very last breath David Bowie and she "were utterly complimentary and as passionate as ever," and speaks of her widowhood thusly: "The struggle is real, but so is God."

Postscript

BBC News reported that David Bowie's will provides that his estate (valued at about $100 million) be divided as follows: half to his wife Iman and the rest to his son and daughter, with some minor provisions for his personal assistant ($2 million) and a former nannie for his son ($1 million).

Bowie's will, filed in a Manhattan court under his given

name, David Robert Jones, provided that his cremated ashes be scattered in a Buddhist ritual in Bali.

Also, in a previously unreleased interview for *60 Minutes* made in 2003, Bowie made the following remarks:

> "I was never fond of my voice. I never thought of myself as a singer. I thought I wrote songs, that is what I was best at doing. i would much preferred other people sing my songs."

I personally find it remarkable that David Bowie, with his flair for the theatrical and the dramatic, says with a straight face that he would have preferred staying out of the limelight, but there you have it. *60 Minutes* certainly caught Bowie acting engaged and relaxed during his interviews. Some of his last remarks are more consistent with the persona of Bowie as a family man:

> "I'm comfortable with the idea of getting old... life has gotten better than it ever has been; i feel comfortable with it ...I'm really very thankful...I have a great wonderful domestic life...I consider myself a very lucky guy, I really do..."

Sources

http://time.com/4175275/david-bowie-name-change/cite

Time Magazine, David Bowie: His Life on Earth, an 80-page, fully illustrated commemorative edition.

http://www.cnn.com/2016/01/12/entertainment/david-bowie-iman-feat/index.html

John Lyons, *America in the British Imagination: 1945 to the Present,* Palgrave Macmillan US, 2013.

http://grantland.com/features/chuck-klosterman-alex-pappademas-david-bowie-career/

http://www.rollingstone.com/music/news/david-bowie-dead-at-69-20160111?page=4. Source for Rolling Stone magazine's obituarity for Bowie.

https://heavy.com/entertainment/2016/01/angela-bowie-david-ex-wife-first-mary-barnett-married-who-age-height-to-kids-mother/Source for Angela's remarks on her marriage to David.

http://articles.chicagotribune.com/1993-01-25/features/9303172042_1_david-bowie-angela-bowie-divorce

http://www.cbsnews.com/news/david-bowies-unaired-60-minutes-interviews. Source for posthumous quotes by Bowie.

www.bbc.com/news/entertainment-arts-35449063

The Crossroads of
Eric Clapton

ERIC CLAPTON'S VERSION of the song "Crossroads" describes the guitar legend's life, and his life's work. Clapton's life work is not just playing the guitar; it includes being a recovering drug addict and alcoholic. Without a sturdy recovery from his addictions, the seventy-seven year-old would not be able to perform at the remarkable level he is at today.

Technically, Crossroads isn't Clapton's song. It was written in the 1930's by Robert Johnson. Johnson has been Clapton's muse throughout the six decades Clapton has been playing guitar in public. Clapton co-authored the book *Discovering Robert Johnson*, in which he described Johnson as

> *"...the most important blues musician who ever lived. He was true, absolutely, to his own vision, and as deep as I have gotten into the music over the last 30 years, I have never found anything more deeply soulful than Robert Johnson. His music remains the most powerful cry that I think you can find in the human voice, really. ... it seemed to echo something I had always felt."*

By the time Clapton was born (1945) Johnson had already been dead for seven years. Very little is known about Johnson's life, which lends it an aura of mystery. We know he grew up black and poor in the rural south during the Great Depression. His musical career consisted of traveling from town to town looking for places to play his guitar. Often it was the street corner, with Johnson living off donations to his cause.

As Johnson traveled, he became involved with different women. He died in 1938 at the age of twenty-seven in Greenwood, Mississippi. Seems a jealous boyfriend poisoned Johnson, who died in painful agony. Recognition of his artistry came decades later when Bob Dylan, the Rolling Stones, Jimi Hendrix, and the Allman Brothers recorded Johnson's songs and sang his praises. Many of Johnson's songs are now blues standards – including Cross Road Blues, made famous by Eric Clapton's live version (Crossroads) when he was with Cream.

Outwardly, Clapton's journey to the Crossroads seemed very different from Robert Johnson. Eric was raised in Surrey, a county just south of London, by a middle-class family veiling an awkward truth: Eric had been born out of wedlock to a teenage mother. The family's solution was to create a fiction: Eric's grandparents pretended to be his birth parents, and Eric's mother pretended to be his sister. The deception was deliberate and total. Eric grew up believing a lie.

When Eric finally found out his sister was really his mother, his personality changed. He became moody and remote. He began failing at school. He had been lied to by the people he trusted the most. Now he felt different from everyone else. Like Robert Johnson, Eric Clapton didn't know who his father was.

At this time blues music came across the sea from

America and acted like a transfusion to teenaged Eric. He began playing along to blues records with his guitar. He became a more defiant outsider, living almost exclusively in his interior world of music and the history of music, particularly black America's blues and rock music. His appetite for his new world was voracious. He had to know everything he could, not only the music but the musicians: B.B. King, Muddy Waters, Buddy Guy - and Robert Johnson.

It is easy to see how blues music would appeal to a tortured, troubled teenager. The blues shine a light on the most painful aspects of being human - lost love, jealousy, betrayal - and then exorcises these agonies of life in an emotional musical catharsis. Eric's personal demons may have attracted him to blues music, but the real story is how it revealed his musical gift: an ability to recreate the emotion of the blues singers with a fluid, evocative immediacy through his guitar.

Young Clapton quickly learned the blues musical catechism. What transformed his music was his ability to meld his own passions with the suffering of the musicians he listened to, and express both in the fluent language of the electric guitar. After a few intense years of learning his new craft, Clapton moved to London, joined a blues band called the Yardbirds, and made a name for himself. In short order he was a world-class musician and co-founder of rock's first supergroup: Cream.

Cream was a great band with a short shelf life. Clapton went through a couple other bands before he formed Derek and the Dominos. The Dominos, with an assist from Duane Allman, recorded the seminal blues-rock album, *Layla and Other Assorted Love Songs*. Layla was the code name for Patty Boyd, George Harrison's wife and the object of Clapton's affections. The record and Clapton's bid for Patty failed. The Dominos broke up, Patty and George did not, and Clapton developed a heroin addiction.

By the end of the 1970's Clapton had kicked heroin, released a solo album that established his talents as a composer and singer, and married Patty Boyd. Dreams do come true, but they don't last forever. Eric stayed off heroin but began drinking heavily. In 1982 Clapton admitted he was an alcoholic and entered treatment. Of this he said:

"In the lowest moments of my life, the only reason I didn't commit suicide was that I knew I wouldn't be able to drink anymore if I was dead. It was the only thing I thought was worth living for, and the idea that people were about to try and remove me from alcohol was so terrible that I drank and drank and drank, and they had to practically carry me into the clinic."

There were some relapse years but by the end of the 1980's Clapton was sober. And divorced. He and Patty loved each other but just couldn't make it work. The 90's brought more hard times. Clapton's good friend and fellow guitarist Stevie Ray Vaughan was killed in a helicopter accident while touring with Clapton. Then Clapton's four-year-old son Conor fell to his death from a New York City apartment window. Here was a daunting crossroads: how would Clapton respond?

He wrote a song about Conor called "Tears in Heaven" that won a Grammy. And he established a drug and rehabilitation center on the Caribbean Island of Antigua. Clapton named it the Crossroads Centre.

Crossroads Centre is a non-profit residential drug and alcohol rehabilitation center that provides subsidized care for some of the poorest people of the Caribbean who cannot afford the help. A foundation was established to provide "scholarships" for these people and for people throughout the world. Crossroads Centre's biggest fundraiser has been Eric Clapton.

In 1999 Clapton auctioned off 100 of his guitars for a cool $5 million dollars, which he donated to Crossroads Centre. A few years later Clapton began hosting the Crossroads Guitar Festival, an invitation-only event for those guitarists Clapton deems to be the cream of the cream. The festivals have raised millions of dollars for the Crossroads Centre and showcased many remarkable artists. Held every three years, the most recent one was last spring at Madison Square Garden.

In October 2007, Eric's autobiography was published. It was a best seller and was translated into twelve different languages. Clapton talked frankly about his addictions to alcohol and heroin, and more:

> *"I found a pattern in my behavior that had been repeating itself for years, decades even. Bad choices were my specialty, and if something honest and decent came along, I would shun it or run the other way.*
>
> *"All I am certain of right now is that I don't want to go anywhere, and that's not bad for someone who always used to run."*

Eric Clapton's guitar playing has always been remarkable. Now it appears Eric the person is becoming as remarkable as his artistry: or are they finally one and the same?

The most recent crossroads for Eric Clapton concerned the COVID pandemic. Eric got the vaccination and had a serious physical reaction to it. This made him opposed to vaccine mandates, which are not a "one size fits all" situation. So Eric has been outspoken on this issue, and the fact that he contacted COVID even after getting the jab.

Clapton is not opposed to vaccinations for COVID. What he does oppose is the refusal to consider that mandated vaccinations are not always the best cure for COVID, particularly for those who have had the virus and so have acquired a higher natural immunity from COVID than what can be provided for by jabs. Clapton is still touring at age seventy-seven. He had to cancel some concerts when he contracted COVID. The last word for now is that Clapton seems to be recovering well and is looking forward to touring again.

Sources

http://crossroadsguitarfestival.com/

http://www.crossroadsantigua.org/

Eric Clapton's official website, http://www.ericclapton.com/

Eric Clapton: The Autobiography, Century, 2007. This is the source for all the quotations from EC used in this article.

The Redemption of Mickey Rourke

WHAT CAN YOU say about a guy who gives up a glamorous and lucrative acting career portraying a male heartthrob to getting punched in the face for a living? You can say he is Mickey Rourke and he does things his way.

The flip side of fame has a rude way of making celebs own their own manure, or at least make it obvious what they are not owning. It's tough growing up, especially growing up in public. We'll see how that applies to Rourke in a moment.

First, let's note "Mickey" is a nickname, a nod to Rourke's Irish descent. German, French, and Scottish blood also flowed through his veins when he was born on September 16, 1952, and given the Christian name Philip Andre Rourke Junior. The senior Rourke was an amateur bodybuilder who deserted his family when his namesake was six. Senior never returned.

Mickey's mom , Annette Rourke, remarried a tough Miami Beach cop named Eugene Addis. Then she moved Mickey and his siblings Joey and Patricia from New York to Florida to live with Addis and his five children (four boys).

Rourke said he learned to box at the Miami Boy's Club. He liked it enough to pursue an amateur career. In 1969 he got to spar with former World Welterweight champion Luis Rodriguez. Later Rourke said Rodriguez concussed him. It would not be the last concussion in Rourke's boxing career, which spanned decades.

Rourke claims to have had an impressive amateur record: 27 victories, 3 defeats, and 17 victories by knockout. Some Internet sources detail his career by opponent and outcome. The one I saw had a remarkable number of extremely fast victories – knockouts in less than one minute of the first round. There are three reasons for such a record. One: Mickey was a helluva puncher. Two: his opponents were saps. Three: stay tuned for the third reason.

Meanwhile a friend of Rourke was directing a play and needed someone to replace an actor who quit the production. Rourke filled in and discovered he liked acting. It was rumored he also liked burglary, so Mickey may have had extra motivation to borrow money from sister Patricia to go to New York (or flee Miami Beach) to take up acting.

Fate was smiling when Rourke stumbled into an audition for the elite Actor's Studio. Famed director Elia Kazan called Rourke's performance "the best audition in 30 years." Mickey started taking private acting lessons. He recalled, "I liked that you could escape who you were and be someone else, someone smarter, tougher."

After some television exposure in the 1970's and a couple of bit parts in movies, Rourke got his first break, a small one, as the arsonist in *Body Heat*. Next year there was a bigger break, as Boogie Sheftell in *Diner*. An ensemble cast did not prevent Rourke from getting special attention for his role as a compulsive gambler and con man who hits on his friend's wife, then regrets it and backs away before consummation. Rourke was named Best Supporting Actor by the National Society of Film Critics.

Roles kept coming. There was *Rumblefish* by Francis

Ford Coppola, then *The Pope of Greenwich Village* in 1984. Later Rourke would say of this film:

> "It was the most fun I've ever had on a movie. It was one of the happiest times in my life. I was living in New York, and I really enjoyed acting at the time...it's funny because that was the time when I went downhill."

Well, not quite - at least not so anyone would notice. Rourke's star seemed instead to be steadily rising. His first lead role was in *9 1/2 Weeks*, a monotonous eroticom with Kim Basinger. The movie was trashed critically but was very popular for the kinky sexuality. Mickey Rourke was now a sex symbol.

He also had serious chops as an actor, which he displayed in his role as alcoholic writer Charles Bukowski in *Barfly.* Then came *Year of the Dragon,* and *Angel Heart*, another controversial movie praised by critics and nominated for multiple awards. Acting alongside Robert DeNiro and Lisa Bonet, Rourke carried the movie with his convincing portrayal of a seedy low-life detective. American audiences freaked out over a short sex scene between Rourke and Bonet that featured blood dripping from the walls. Audiences in Europe weren't as squeamish. Europeans loved Rourke, especially the French.

Perhaps Rourke's fans loved him more than he loved himself. At the high point of his career Rourke began making curious decisions. Like going from sex symbol to saint by starring in a docudrama of St. Francis of Assisi. Then there was *Wild Orchid*, a disaster savaged by critics. Another box office and critical bomb was 1991's *Harley Davidson and the Marlboro Man.* Even the title makes you wince.

What's more, Rourke seemed to be mailing in his roles,

relying on his trademark smirk instead of taking his role to heart and performing. So why was the global heart throb and critically acclaimed actor sleep walking through duds? And why was he turning down plum roles in monster movies like *Platoon, Beverly Hills Cop, Top Gun, 48 Hours, The Silence of the Lambs,* and *Pulp Fiction?* It is even said that Dustin Hoffman called Rourke to offer him a part in *Rain Man,* and Rourke never returned Hoffman's call.

Rumors started that Rourke was "a nightmare" to work with, even "very dangerous." During the shooting of one movie Rourke brought his bodyguards to the set. They were (real) Hell's Angels who intimidated cast and crew. The consequences for this behavior were that actors (like Nicole Kidman) refused to work with Rourke solely because of his reputation.

Years later Rourke admitted:

"I thought my acting talent transcended the business of films. I never had a game plan for my career. I didn't have the tools for that. I became arrogant and self-destructive. I fought everyone cause I thought that was a kind of strength, but it became my weakness."

During this period of his life Rourke seemed unable to rise to the challenge: to seize a major role in a major movie, devote himself to his craft, silence the critics and regain his self-respect. It was an opportunity any actor would love, because it doesn't happen very often. When it happened to Rourke in 1991, he declined the challenge to take his acting career to the next level. Instead, at the age of thirty-nine, he became a professional boxer.

Rourke went back to Miami Beach to train. He even had world class trainer Freddie Roach in his corner (along with a couple of Hell's Angels). Rourke's plan was to have about sixteen fights, which would lead to a world championship bout he planned to win. "I was fighting guys 15 years younger than me," Rourke explained. "But I won 10 of 12 fights and had two draws."

Actually, there were eight fights. Rourke won six (4 by KO) and had two draws. Sounds good on paper. In reality he was booed in the ring when he waltzed to one draw. The *Miami Herald* called his fights a farce. *World Boxing Magazine* asked, "Mickey Rourke: Acting Like a Boxer, or Boxing Like an Actor?"

His boxing career was financially lucrative because of his celebrity status. His opposition was padded and carefully chosen, but Rourke still paid a heavy price. His ribs, toe, and nose were fractured, and his cheekbone was compressed. Getting hit repeatedly in the face is a surefire way to lose heart throb looks. Rourke's tongue was split as well, which did not improve his diction.

Then there was the short-term memory loss. Rourke was starting to act punch drunk. His neurologist said Mickey wouldn't have a brain left if he didn't retire immediately. Rourke retired.

Sometimes Rourke talks about his boxing career in inflated terms, as if he could have had a championship fight except for his health. For Rourke, as for many others, truth and fantasy intertwine. No less a Miami Beach authority than Angelo Dundee declares Rourke never had one amateur fight in Miami in his entire life. The National Golden Glove Association say it is "unlikely" Mickey fought as an amateur, but they did not keep records that far back. Yet if Golden Gloves didn't keep records, where do all the Internet boxing records come from?

Whatever Mickey's boxing history was or wasn't, in 1994 his face, body, and mind were a mess. Then his second wife, an actress and heroin addict, split up with him. Rourke hit bottom, an experience he sometimes describes with brutal honesty, and at other times in a glamorizing or self-pitying way.

"I lost the house, the wife, the credibility, the entourage. I lost my soul. I was alone ... The only thing I could afford was a shrink, so that's where my money went. Three times a week for the first two years. The year after that, twice a week and now I'm down to once a week. I've only missed two appointments in six years."

The only thing he could afford was a shrink? Psychiatrists charge $3-500 an hour, and Rourke saw one three times a week? For years? Well, then, he had some serious money with him. Money doesn't cure everything, and Mickey was in acute distress. The suffering continued when he started on the plastic surgery circuit to repair his damaged face.

Rourke ran into a quack who grossly disfigured face. He looked appalling – seriously terrible. Several subsequent surgeries were necessary to undo the quack work. Other procedures followed over the years, leading to assertions that Rourke was "addicted" to cosmetic surgery.

Mickey was out of commission for about twelve long years. He lived with his dogs and became a dog rescuer. He credits his Catholic faith with keeping him alive.

"I talked to my priest a lot. I used to have to call him or the shrink when there was an explosion, because I was really good at not talking to anybody until there was an explosion. My priest is this cool Italian from New York. We go down to his basement and he opens the wine. We smoke a cigarette and I have my confession. He sends me upstairs to do my Hail Marys.

"I mean, I'm no Holy Joe, but I have a strong belief. If I wasn't Catholic, I would have blown my brains out. I would pray to God. I would say, "Please, can you send me just a little bit of daylight?" He talked me out of it, and we started meeting. His name is Father Pete and he lives in New York. Father Pete put me back on the right track."

With the help of his shrink, Father Pete, and his dogs, Rourke made it through the dark times. He realized he wanted to act again. It was several years before he could get a decent role, much less get back his credibility on the screen. But make it back he did, in 2008's *The Wrestler*, a sweet, tough redemption story Rourke makes ring true. He portrayed a washed up, over the hill professional wrestler named Randy "The Ram" Robinson. Too old for the bright lights, Robinson can't forget his glory days, and can't face his bleak, unrewarding job at a supermarket. The movie ends during Robinson's last match. Alonso Duralde, of MSNBC, said, "Rourke's work transcends mere stunt-casting; his performance is a howl of pain that seems to come from a very real place."

Rourke won a Golden Globe award and an Academy Award nomination for Best Actor. His career was revitalized, and he had his self-respect back. "I didn't think I'd come back to this level ever again," Rourke admitted. "I hoped I would, but I thought too much time had gone by." Perhaps there is always enough time to grow up and realize you are okay the way you are; that you don't have to act like someone you are not to be worthy.

Perhaps life has taught Rourke the real way to prove you are a tough guy is not to hang out with Hell's Angels or have boxing matches. The real way to prove you are a tough guy is by taking everything life gives you and hanging in there: suffering on a bed of coals until the cup of suffering has been drained. Then either by grace or the slow grinding of the Dharma wheel, life changes: the sun shines again on smiling, loving faces.

After *The Wrestler* Rourke starred as a villain in *Iron*

Man 2 in 2010. He was also featured in *The Expendables* (2010) and *Immortals* (2011). Then came the crown for his suffering years: a space on the Hollywood Walk of Fame. It was an honor that by now Mickey Rourke could truly appreciate.

What has Rourke learned?

"I learned to keep a lid on that little man inside me with two hatchets," he said. "It's not hard to do since the repercussions are so severe. I learned I had to conduct myself in a professional manner. I had lost my career because I had put the blame everywhere but where it belonged. On me. I didn't want to make the same mistake again.

"You know, actors live in a constant state of fear that it'll all slip away. You want to earn respect in your old age. You want to walk into a restaurant and have people say: 'There's Mickey Rourke. He was great in *"The Wrestler."*' You don't want them jumping out of windows."

Sounds like a lesson well learned and well earned. Good on you Mickey.

Sources

http://www.imdb.com/name/nm0000620/ -

http://www.theguardian.com/film/2008/nov/23/mickey-rourke-interview

http://www.biography.com/people/mickey-rourke-9465337

Requiem for a Werewolf
(An Accidental Tribute to Warren Zevon)

ONE LATE SPRING afternoon I came home playing a cassette tape of Warren's song "Empty Handed Heart," and singing along on a descant he shared with Linda Ronstadt to close out the tune.

The song was beautiful beyond words, a beauty far above the illegal substances humming in my body. The day was beautiful. Even I was beautiful. It was all so wonderful I started shouting "Glorious!" in the parking lot, attracting attention as I tended to do in those days. I followed Warren's career and emulated his debauched lifestyle: I was young and eminently stupid enough to pull it off.

Empty Handed Heart *is* a glorious song, one of many jewels in the body of work from a man born as Warren Zivotofsky: Warren's ancestors were Ukrainian Jews who, upon landing in Brooklyn changed their last name to Zevon.

Warren had a star crossed childhood. The Zevons were not rich, but they were able to send Warren to piano lessons with Igor Stravinsky. On the other hand, Warren's parents didn't tell him they were getting divorced. One day Dad was gone, and Elmer the roofer moved in to live with Mom. Elmer and Warren hated each other, and Warren got even with Elmer by delving into his liquor cabinet whenever he could. Music and alcohol paired up early on in Warren's life.

I don't like all of Warren's songs, but invariably there were several songs on each album striking for their beauty, lyrical eloquence, or hysterical humor. Perhaps it is Zevon's humor that sticks with me the most. His wit was by turns acerbic and slapstick – sometimes both at the same time. Check out some song titles: Life'll Kill Ya; Things to do in Denver when you're Dead; I Was in the House When the House Burned Down; Detox Mansion (a reference to Warren's drug rehab);or the riotous "Gorilla You're a Desperado", a satire of James Taylor. Zevon harbored a firm dislike of Taylor for reasons that are only obscure after all these years.

Warren had some close calls with death during his "*Dirty Life and Times*" (the sub-title of a biography of Zevon by his former wife Crystal Zevon, who remained his friend). Warren could have and perhaps should have died several times during his life. His failure to expire was not for want of trying.

Zevon was a raving alcoholic who never met a drug or a pill he didn't like. He had a fondness for large handguns, and when he got too insanely drunk or too addled on Darvon or Percocet or any number of drugs legal or otherwise he would – in a rare lucid moment – manacle himself in a corner so that he wouldn't hurt anyone, or himself.

"I got to be Jim Morrison a lot longer than he did," Zevon bragged in 2002, shortly after finding he had only months to live, courtesy of inoperable cancer. His peers considered Warren a musical genius. Critically acclaimed throughout his career, popular success eluded him until his death – with one exception. A little ditty Warren knocked off in less than an hour called Werewolves of London became his only hit song, a fact that annoyed Warren intensely. Proof, perhaps, that God always has the last laugh.

In 1987 I saw Zevon in concert after we had both given up alcohol and drugs. Warren headlined at the Orpheum Theater in downtown Minneapolis on a warm September night. He was energetic, often switching from guitar to piano, and back again. He seemed good natured and happy to have the opportunity to entertain his audience.

Zevon's concert took place barely a mile away from the Minneapolis Metrodome, where the Minnesota Twins and the Atlanta Braves met for Game One of the baseball World Series the same night of the concert. For an encore Warren came on stage with a Twins jersey on – and announced the Twins had just won Game One. Then he launched into "Werewolves", and we all danced. It was a happy night.

Zevon seemed outwardly content with his new life of sobriety, but beneath the surface his addiction to alcohol was replaced by an addiction to sex that lasted for the rest of his life. He also suffered from obsessive compulsive disorder. A particular quirk concerned bad luck or bad omens, which could be revealed only by asking "Is it bad luck?" not once, but twice.

So, Warren was a tortured artist whether he was drunk or sober. When drugs were off the menu there was still sex and rock and roll to fall back on. Zevon also found occasional solace in religion. His first wife Crystal remembers how she and Warren used to sit in a church in Spain and hold hands.

Warren told her he was going to convert to Catholicism, and they would have a dozen babies. He sounded serious.

If religion had the power to periodically puncture Zevon's sardonic wit, at other times it was the court of last resort. In 2000 Zevon lost his voice right before a show. As he tells the story: "something told me to find a church. I walked right in on a mass in progress, left $100 in the poor box and prayed to sing. It was very bright outside and I felt light...The show was good. I know why. Peace be with you."

Anyone tempted to canonize Zevon should hear the other side of the story. He could be an absolute bastard, selfish and cruel to the point of inhumanity. He used people to further his career and then abandoned them. He abused his wife and family, once kicking them out of the house on Christmas morning. He persevered in his craft for decades, but perseverance seemed always to duel with chaos and adversity in his personal life, almost as if suffering was a necessary ingredient of the perseverance – or vice versa.

Warren eventually landed a regular gig as head musician on the David Letterman Show, which is probably how most people remember him (aside from "Werewolves"). In 2002 when Zevon was diagnosed with terminal cancer Letterman devoted a show to Warren. As the vultures circled Warren started to get a taste of the fame that had eluded him all his life. He went into the studio to make one last album, the monster album, the best seller he would probably not live to see. This struck him as hilarious.

He grew weaker by the hour. There was real doubt whether Warren would live long enough to finish the album. "It's a sin not to try to stay alive," Warren told Bruce Springsteen during a session. What Zevon did not say was that he was drinking liquid morphine and chasing it down with $500 bottles of scotch. Impending death did what life could not – it knocked Warren off the sobriety wagon. Yet death did not shake his quiet undercurrent of religiosity. According to a friend, "his belief in God was unwavering. Never once did Warren question why this was happening to him."

Zevon finished the album and called it "The Wind." He lived long enough to be a grandfather when his daughter gave birth to twin boys. After the delivery Warren and Crystal went to the hospital chapel so Warren could "thank the Big Guy in the sky." He died not much later, on September 7, 2003.

Warren Zevon left behind a lot of people who had grown to love him over the good years and bad years. I still listen to Warren, and I have good memories of the good years and bad years I had growing up and growing older with him. For every lyric of his that makes my heart ache there is another one that gives me a belly laugh. May God bless and keep you, you damned old werewolf.

Warren Zivotofsky, *Requiescat in pacem*.

Source

The source for this article is a biography of Warren Zevon written by his ex-wife, Crystal Zevon, entitled I'll Sleep When I'm Dead: The Dirty Life and Times of Warren Zevon, published in 2007 by Harper Collins Publisher, New York.

The reference in the subtitle of this article to "An Accidental Tribute" is a nod to Zevon's song "Accidentally Like A Martyr", where the hurt gets worse as the heart gets harder.

How Cat Stevens became Yusuf Islam and Came Back Again

THIS IS A story about a man whose different names marked significant parts of his artistic and spiritual life.

He is now known as Yusuf Islam, or Yusuf, a devout Muslim slowly opening himself up again to the West. There he is better known as Cat Stevens, an intensely personal folk artist who had several hit music albums in the 1970's. Then he converted to Islam and abandoned his music career. In time Yusuf Islam's new religion made him notorious, even anathema to Western media, Western society, even Western law. And the feeling was decidedly mutual.

But before Yusuf, before Cat Stevens, there was a tiny infant baptized as Stephen Demetre Georgiou on July 21, 1948, in London, England. Stephen was the youngest of three children (older sister Anita and brother David) born to Stavros and Ingrid (nee Wickman) Georgiou. Dad was a Greek Cypriot and Mom was a Swedish Baptist.

The religiously and culturally diverse pair ran a restaurant called the Moulin Rouge on the West End of London and lived with their family in an apartment above the restaurant. Stephen and his siblings waited tables and washed dishes.

Although Stephen was raised in the Greek Orthodox faith, he attended school at a Roman Catholic parish. Neither religion had kind words for Islam, a religion and culture they accused of heinous crimes against innocent Christian citizens.

Stephen was drawn to the piano in his parent's apartment. He taught himself to play, and at age eight escaped into music when his parents divorced. He learned guitar and sometimes went up to the roof of the family apartment to play and sing the songs he was writing. At times music echoed back to him from nearby Denmark Street. Everyone from the Rolling Stones to the Sex Pistols had played or recorded on Denmark Street.

Stephen cites early influences as the Beatles, Bob Dylan, and the musical West Side Story. By age seventeen (1965) he was playing in coffee houses under the name Steven Adams. One year later he signed a contract with Decca Records and underwent another name change, this time to Cat Stevens. Why? Well, his girlfriend said he had eyes like a cat, but mostly because, as the artist himself put it, "I couldn't imagine anyone going to the record store and asking for 'that Steven Demetre Georgiou album.'"

Stevens and Decca released his first album, "Matthew and Son," in 1966. Two singles from the album reached the UK top ten, and so did the album. A follow up album contained "The First Cut Is The Deepest," a song Stevens later sold for $50. The song made millions for four other artists, including Cheryl Crow and Rod Stewart.

Just when Steven's star began to shine, he contracted tuberculosis, and dropped out of the music scene for two years. It is his bent to put a spiritual meaning to events, and here is how he viewed his TB diagnosis:

"I felt I was on the brink of death. At the same time, I had incredible hope. I kind of made the best of it as much as I could. Now I had a break I could review myself and decide where I wanted to go and not necessarily where my agent felt I should go." (see Sources for citation).

In fact, he was on the brink of death, and recovered only slowly. The next two years were spent becoming a vegetarian, taking up meditation, studying metaphysics – oh yes, and writing about forty songs. When he got back in the studio the songs became albums, and Cat Stevens became a worldwide mega star.

The albums: Tea for the Tillerman, Teaser and the Firecat, Catch Bull at Four, and others, vaulted Stevens into super stardom as the quintessential sensitive singer song-writer. He joined the ranks of James Taylor, Joni Mitchell, and Carly Simon, who had a relationship with Stevens and wrote two songs about him. One, "Anticipation" (also known as "the ketchup song") has the great line: "These are the good old days."

Stevens had his share of singles too: "Father and Son," "Wild World," "Peace Train," "Morning Has Broken," "Moon Shadow," "Where Do the Children Play," "Tuesday's Dead," "But I Might Die Tonight," "The Hurt," and "Miles From Nowhere," among others. Unlike his contemporaries, how-ever, Cat Stevens did the artwork for all his album covers.

Tuberculosis marked one turning point in Steven's life, and almost drowning marked another. He was swimming in the Pacific Ocean, off the coast of Malibu, when the current prevented him from returning to shore.

"Suddenly I was petrified," he recalled. "I thought: 'This might be it.' I said: 'God, if you save me, I'll work for you.' It was without hesitation that I knew that, instinctively, there was a power that could help me. And then a little wave, you know, came behind me — a little wave, it wasn't very big. But it was that miraculous moment when suddenly the tide was going in my favor. I had my energy; I could swim back. I was on land. I was alive. Wow, what next?" (see Sources for citation).

Next was another sea change (pun unintended) in the life of Cat Stevens. Open as never before to spiritual currents, he began reading a book his brother David gave him for his birthday. It was the Koran.

"This was before Islam was a headline," Yusuf says. "The Iranian Revolution wasn't even on the horizon. I felt like I was discovering something that was an amazing and immense secret." For Stevens, the Koran had answers for questions he had been asking for years. In December 1977 he formally became a Muslim and changed his name to Yusuf Islam. Could he be a Muslim and a pop star at the same time?

"Yeah, when it came to trying to balance you know, this knowledge, this discovery (Islam), with my lifestyle (pop star), you know, I've been singing about trying to find who I am. Now I've found out, do I have to keep singing? I mean, that was the question."

The answer was No. Yusuf sold all his guitars and gave the proceeds to charity. He used the royalties still pouring in (he sold an estimated 6 million albums) to establish the first Muslim school in England. Then he started the Small Kindness charity helping orphans around the world.

He participated in an arranged marriage to Fawzia Ali and began a family with her (they now have five children). Islam stayed out of the spotlight for a decade. Then the spotlight found him.

British author Salmon Rushdie wrote a book called "The Satanic Verses" that was highly critical of Islam. In 1989 Iran's Ayatollah Khomeini issued a fatwa calling for Rushdie's death. It was natural for the press to seek out Britain's most famous Muslim for his reaction. Yusuf told an audience at London's Kingston University:

"[Rushdie] must be killed. The Quran makes it clear: If someone defames the prophet, then he must die." Later Yusuf would soften the blow a bit, but even when he sugars the pill he is speaking as a devout Muslim – a tongue alien to free speech loving Westerners:

> "I'm a firm believer in the law. I was never a sup-
> porter of the *fatwa* [against Rushdie], but people
> don't want to hear that because they keep saying
> that I believe in the law of blasphemy. All I'm saying
> is, how can you deny the Third Commandment? It's
> an Islamic principle that you must follow the law of
> the land where you reside." (see Sources for citation)

Yusuf was slammed publicly as an intolerant Muslim by the Western press, a perception that had legs, as they say in the media. To this day Rushdie and Britain's literary establishment have not forgiven Yusuf for his remarks.

In America his songs stopped getting airplay. Even though Yusuf publicly condemned the terrorism of 9/11/2001 he was put on a "no-fly" list. In 2004 Islam was flying to Washington D.C. to participate in a charity. He was pulled off the flight and denied entry into America.

Then Yusuf – the man who wrote "Peace Train" – was accused of funding the terrorist Hamas group. He denied doing so knowingly, a response seen as weak and equivocating by his critics, which by this time were many.

Then there was another turning point, a "Father and Son" moment - except now Yusuf was the father. His son, who had been trying to get dad to play guitar for years, pointedly brought a guitar home. After his family had gone to bed it was just Yusuf and the guitar staring at each other. He recalled:

"When everybody's asleep and nobody's watching, I pick it up ... and lo and behold, I still know where to put my fingers. Out comes this music. I said, 'Maybe I've got another job to do.'" (See Sources for citations).

In doing his 'job' Yusuf found himself between two worlds. On the one hand there was a mistrustful, baffled West who did not understand or appreciate Yusuf's conversion to Islam. On the other hand, there was a mistrustful, baffled Muslim community who saw no positive religious purpose in Yusuf picking up his guitar again. Nevertheless, in 2006, after twenty-eight years of musical silence, Yusuf released his album An Other Cup. Of it he said:

"The cup is there to be filled...with whatever you want to fill it with. For those people looking for Cat Stevens, they'll probably find him in this record. If you want to find Yusuf, go a bit deeper, you'll find him." (See Sources for citation)

An Other Cup received positive reviews. Later that same year Yusuf earned an ASCAP award for "The First Cut is the Deepest." In 2007 Yusuf was awarded three times by three different bodies (an Echo award, an honorary doctorate by Exeter University, and the Mediterranean Prize for Peace) for his work increasing understanding between Islam and the West.

In 2008 Yusuf was nominated for induction into the Songwriters Hall of Fame. He continued to make music, releasing two other records after An Other Cup. On subsequent records he has quietly dropped the "Islam" from his name, so musically he is now known as Yusuf.

Fast forward to 2014, and Yusuf/Cat Stevens is being inducted into the Rock and Roll Hall of Fame. Yusuf the gray headed sensitive singer songwriter is totally overshadowed by Kiss, and Nirvana's reunion, and the usual last-minute craziness of rock and roll.

Yusuf gives a gracious acceptance speech that does not touch on religion or politics. Then, almost unnoticed, he sits down and starts playing his guitar.

The buzzed crowd is there for Nirvana, not some creaky gray head thumbing an old folk song. Then something starts to build. The singer's voice is focused, intensely present. Suddenly the lyrics are happening in your heart. Yusuf is singing "Father and Son", and he delivers the climactic couplet like a rifle crack. Then the song ends as it started, quietly. But now the crowd is intently quiet, suddenly as present as the singer.

"Peace Train" had to be the next song, and it was. Yusuf's body relaxed and he strummed away as a gospel choir boomed and soared behind him. The audience rose as one, arms waving, singing along to every word. "It was glorious," Yusuf said later. "It was great to sing without any barriers..."

Speaking of peace and no barriers, Yusuf has this to say about religious conflict:

"I don't think that God sent us prophets and books to fight about these books and these prophets. But they were telling us how to live together. If we ignore those teachings ... whichever faith you belong, you profess, then I think we'll be finding ourselves in an even deeper mess." (see Sources for citations for this quote and the following quote)

And for today's threat to peace that ISIS brings, Yusuf points out: "The positive side is that it has brought together these factional voices to say in unison that [ISIS] has nothing to do with Islam."

From peace in the world to peace inside, here is Yusuf/ Cat Stevens (as he now bills himself at concerts) on himself:

"When you've been running for so long, you might realize you've run too far. There comes a time to say, 'Hang on. I've lost my way a little bit.'"

Can't we all say that sometimes?

Sources

http://www.bbc.co.uk/radio2/r2music/documentaries/cat-stevens.shtml Source for Yusuf's remarks on his An Other Cup album.

http://www.biography.com/people/cat-stevens-16548027citation

http://www.rollingstone.com/music/features/yusuf-islams-golden-years-cat-stevens-on-islam-and-his-return-to-music-20150113 Source for remarks about Rushdie and Islamic law.

http://www.majicat.com/articles/disc72_cat.htm

http://www.cbsnews.com/news/yusuf-islam-reflects-on-his-return/Source for Yusuf's remarks on world peace and ISIS.

The Violent Life And Death of Bruiser Brody

IN THE REAL fake world of professional wrestling Bruiser Brody had a reputation as a badass. This was saying something, for professional wrestling is full of alpha males with testosterone oozing out of every pore, muscles bulging, and veins popping. Even among these physical specimens Brody had a reputation as the toughest of the tough. He lived up to his rep, and eventually it cost him his life.

In the beginning he was Frank Goodish, growing up in a Detroit suburb with his parents and three sisters. The girls remember having pillow fights with their only brother. Frank, they all said, was sweet with a devilish streak. His first love was playing football. His sisters remember it was all he talked about doing. Frank never mentioned wrestling; it was not on the Brody family's TV viewing schedule.

In high school Frank played tight end on offense and tackle on defense. He had soft hands that could catch almost any pass, and at 6'4" and 215 pounds he was a ferocious run stopper. Frank received a football scholarship from Iowa State but only lasted a year. He bounced down to Wayne State, and finally to West Texas State, the "island of misfit toys" on the college football circuit. Players with issues went to West Texas. Many of the team's football players went on to become either professional football players or professional wrestlers.

Goodish played with Mercury Morris, who won a Super Bowl with the Miami Dolphins in the 1970's. Other team-mates were Stan Hansen, Ted DiBiase, Bobby Duncum, and Terry Funk (all became professional wrestlers). Funk's dad Dory ran a wrestling promotion in Texas. Frank started attending matches. He was impressed that the Funks and other wrestlers on the circuit were legitimate celebrities. Terry Funk said,

"Frank loved being physical, the camaraderie, and the attention that came from playing football...He was a great football player. Hardnosed and tough. But it was a lark to him. He was nuts back then."

Goodish wanted to major in journalism but got kicked out of West Texas before graduating for disciplinary reasons. He hooked up with a semi-pro football team, the San Antonio Toros, and landed a job with the sports department at the local newspaper. Frank was a decent writer. His nemesis was the typewriter. His huge fingers invariably hit two or three keys at once, trying the patience of an already impatient young man.

Goodish got a tryout with the Washington Redskins, who at the time were being coached by the legendary Vince Lombardi, one of the few people Frank was in awe of. "After working with Lombardi," Frank recalled, "I realized I had the ability to do something in football. It was an education I got too late." Lombardi contracted cancer and died. His replacement cut Goodish from the team. "I was just as fast and tough as all of them," Frank said, "but they had all the fundamentals down cold and I fought trying to learn them." The Redskins tryout was Goodish's fifth and last chance to play football. He failed every time and was honest about it: "I was uncoachable."

Frank returned to San Antonio a failure. He started worked on a loading dock, and lifted weights fanatically. By now he was huge: 6'8" and 300 pounds of solid muscle. He met another lifter, Joe Bednarski, who shared Goodish's passion for football. Bednarski had just started making serious money as a professional wrestler. He called himself Ivan Putski, the Polish Hammer. He was working the Texas circuit with promoter Fritz Von Erich. Frank started training with Bednarski and worked his way into Von Erich's stable of wrestlers. Goodish's love for football transformed into a love of professional wrestling.

Frank had never wrestled before, but he had the physique, the look, and a charisma in the ring and in front of the camera. Equally important, Goodish was finally "coachable." Von Erich took Frank under his wing and taught him the basics. Goodish listened and learned from one of the most experienced men in the business. He improved quickly and was soon in the ring working his way up the card. He ran into his old West Texas State football pal, Stan Hanson, who had been wrestling longer than Frank. They teamed up and won a regional tag team championship.

Frank was very "stiff", that is, he didn't pull his punches or kicks to soften the impact. Professional wrestling is an art form, an athletic ballet where two men tell a story in the ring. Both wrestlers, even though they appear to be in combat with each other, are cooperating in the story telling in order to keep the crowd in a suspended state of disbelief. They are also protecting each other from getting seriously injured. Even though wrestling is fake, the injuries are real, and back then wrestlers had no health insurance. Their bodies were their livelihood.

Goodish learned that instead of competing against his opponent he had to cooperate with him in the ring. But Goodish always wanted his wrestling style to appear real, so he didn't let up on his opponents. Frank's punches and kicks hurt – a lot. He would seriously beat down his opponents. He also learned how to "sell" a punch (act like his opponent hurt him). And he learned when not to sell. Frank's refusal to sell his opponents strength made him enemies of other wrestlers and promoters. He also refused to "job" for other wrestlers (lose to get another wrestler 'over', that is, popular with the fans). His fellow wrestlers thought Frank was selfish and wouldn't cooperate. They were right about the lack of cooperation. From Frank's point of view he was a big man and thought it ridiculous to act like a little man could hurt him. He thought that selling a smaller man made the match seem less real. Wrestling is a business of give and take. Frank wasn't good at that.

Frank began traveling the country. He became a star with his size, charisma, and ability to do promos. Promos are interviews wrestlers do to attract fans to their matches. Frank's charisma and intelligence made for great promos that helped fill houses. Frank worked out his gimmick. He changed his ring name to Bruiser Brody, grew a full beard, grew out his hair down to his shoulders, wore a fur vest, and ran to the ring swinging a metal chain over his head to Led Zeppelin's The Immigrant Song. When Brody hit the ring all hell broke loose.

Goodish's rough, realistic wrestling style, his fierce, wild appearance, and his disregard for anyone's well being made his matches dramatic and intense affairs that often involved blood. "Juicing" occurred when wrestlers secured small bits of taped up razors in their boots, trunks, or elbow pads and used them to nick their foreheads during a match. Any facial cut results in significant blood flow, which of course added to the realism of the match. Brody's forehead became a mass of scar tissue.

He bled a lot, and his opponents bled a lot. Many of

his matches were count outs outside the ring, disqualifications, or double disqualifications. Brody would take his opponent out of the ring and brawl in the stands, causing fans to scatter. Brody had many memorable feuds. The bloodiest was probably with Abdullah the Butcher, a 450 pound Sudanese wrestler with a fondness for carving his initials on his opponents faces with a fork, a repetitive tactic that referees for some reason never smartened up to. Night after night "Abbie" and Brody would gouge away at each other to the delight of the fans. It never seemed to get old.

Something that did get old was Brody's fights with promoters. Goodish had a keen sense of his own worth, and demanded to be compensated at a high level; higher than the other wrestlers on the card. When the promoters disagreed Frank got loud and intimidating. He even beat up some promoters. He was able to get away with this because at this time (the 1980's) there were dozens of promotions across the country, and many more outside the United States. Brody filled houses. He was valuable to promoters. So usually Goodish was accurate about his own worth. But his inflexible refusal to take a penny less than what he thought he earned would end up costing him – and his family – dearly.

After burning bridges with a number of promoters in America, Brody hit Japan and became an instant star: the American Godzilla. He had wild feuds with all the Japanese stars, filled houses and made lots of money. But he alienated so many people the Japanese wrestling promotion fired him. Brody moved to Puerto Rico, definitely a downgrade from Japan. It would be Bruiser Brody's last wrestling event.

The Puerto Rican promotion was run by Carlos Colon. The booker was Jose Gonzales, an old wrestling opponent of Brody. Back in the US Brody had demolished Gonzales in a series of matches. They were "squashes," matches where one wrestler totally dominates the other in a definitive, devastating manner. But in Puerto Rico Gonzales was a star. And as booker, he told the boys who would win, who would lose, and how the card was going to run. Brody was notorious for ignoring booker's directions. He had no respect for Gonzales at all, and was obvious about it.

The story goes that the wrestlers were in the dressing room getting ready for the card. Gonzales asked Brody to come into the shower area for a talk. It was not unusual for bookers to have private conversations with various wrestlers before the matches started. Brody and Gonzales disappeared from view. There were sounds of a scuffle, then groans of pain. Tony Atlas, one of the American wrestlers, ran into the shower area. He saw Gonzales holding a bloody knife. Brody was on the ground. Blood was spurting out of his chest and bubbling, a sign that his lung had been punctured.

An ambulance was called but it took a long time to come. The paramedics couldn't move Brody because of his size. Atlas helped carry him outside to the ambulance. Then there was a delay in getting to the hospital, and another delay in being seen by a doctor. By the time he was tended to Frank Goodish had bled to death. His last words to Atlas were "Tell my wife and son I love them."

Fearing they were next, the American wrestlers fled Puerto Rico. Jose Gonzales and Carlos Colon were wrestling and cultural icons in their country. Americans were definitely outsiders. Gonzales was arrested and charged with murder, a charge that was changed to involuntary homicide. He claimed self-defense and was acquitted. Some of the American wrestlers refused to come to Puerto Rico for the trial. Others received subpoenas to appear only after the trial was over.

The Legendary Charge of the Light Brigade

THE LEGENDARY "CHARGE of the Light Brigade" was an epic military maneuver performed by British cavalrymen during the Crimean War in 1854. The charge inspired Alfred Lord Tennyson's legendary poem "Charge of the Light Brigade", and his famous line: "Into the valley of death rode the six hundred..."

The six hundred were originally one thousand when they landed on the island of Crimea to fight the Russians. By the time of the legendary charge the brigade numbered six hundred seventy-three.

The Light Brigade was a British cavalry unit designed to travel light and fast, with no armor to slow man or horse. Weapons were light as well: lances, sabers, and hand pistols. The Brigade excelled in specialized situations: routing foot soldiers, chasing down fleeing enemy, and performing intelligence, reconnaissance, or scouting duties away from the main force.

In contrast there was the Heavy Brigade, who wore armor, helmets, and used larger cavalry swords. The Heavy Brigade was intended for close combat, including brutal frontal assaults against an enemy.

These two brigades were the only cavalries in the British

army that landed in Crimea. The rest were infantry from England, Scotland, Wales, and even Ireland. Joining the English were 28,000 French infantry.

Why were they fighting the Russians? The Crimean War has sometimes been referred to as a religious war that began when Russia tried to protect its co-religionist's rights in Jerusalem. At that time Jerusalem was under the control of the Ottoman Empire, a toothless rule of benign neglect.

It seems that Catholic and Russian monks were slaughtering each other in Jerusalem over who had control of which sacred sites. Russian Czar Nicholas I demanded the authority to defend the millions of Orthodox Christians in the Ottoman Empire. When this was refused, Nicholas moved his armies into Romania.

This was a direct threat to the Ottoman capital of Constantinople. Russia had the largest army in the world at this time. Constantinople would have been a great prize to acquire for a number of reasons, including giving Russian naval fleets total access to the Mediterranean Sea.

This was a chilling prospect to the British and French, and their ally Turkey. For years they had watched Russia gradually assimilating portions of the declining Ottoman Empire - but taking Constantinople was unacceptable.

So, in a religiously interesting move, Christian England and France prepared to fight Christian Russia to defend a Muslim Empire. Turkey declared war on Russia in October 1853, but when Russian shells defeated Turkish ships, Czar Nicholas ruled the Black Sea, and even ventured into Bulgaria.

This advance was an overstep that provoked Austria's involvement in the quarrel. Nicholas backtracked out of Bulgaria, but too late to avoid war, which was declared by Britain and France in March 1854. To emphasize the declaration they bombarded Odessa, which at that time belonged to Russia.

France and Britain wanted to punish Russia for her boldness by occupying and destroying her main naval base in the Black Sea, located at Sevastopol on the Crimean Peninsula. Both countries dispatched their own fleets to the Black Sea, and soon European soldiers were setting foot on Russian soil.

Britain and France besieged Sevastopol and began bombarding it. After eight days of swallowing cannon balls the Russians attempted to break the siege by attacking Britain's supply base in Balaclava. Along the way they captured four positions on the Causeway Heights just outside Balaclava.

The Russians surged forward but stout defense by Scottish Highlanders and the British Heavy Brigade stopped the Russian flow like a cork in the bottle. The next concern of British commander-in-chief, Lord Fitzroy Somerset Raglan, was to thwart attempts by the Russians to steal English cannons from the Causeway Heights redoubt. It was a perfect job for the Light Brigade, who could sweep in and either scatter the infantry or cut them to pieces before they could move the heavy artillery. The order was placed.

Raglan's order was given to Captain Louis Edward Nolan, who hand delivered the message to cavalry Commander Lieutenant General George Bingham, third Earl of Lucan (called Lucan hereafter). The order was to "advance rapidly to the front ... and try to prevent the enemy carrying away the guns."

Lucan was at a lower position than Raglan and couldn't see any enemies or cannons. Confused, he asked Nolan where he was supposed to attack. According to the story, Nolan gave a vague wave of his arm that Lucan interpreted to refer to a different Russian artillery position one mile away, at the far end of the valley, below Causeway Heights.

Nolan then added something that wasn't in the message:

the Light Brigade was to attack immediately. Lucan ordered the Commander of the Light Brigade, the Earl of Cardigan, to immediately charge the Russian position at the end of the hollow between Causeway Heights and its opposite hill, Fedyukhin Heights. This was the hollow famously dubbed the "Valley of Death" by the poet Tennyson.

The cavalry was mustered with the sense of urgency that follows a direct command to attack at once. The troops made formation and at once broke into a brisk trot along the mile long course to the Russian guns.

Trained eyes immediately noticed the suicidal nature of this mission. The enemy was dug in with many cannons and infantry at the end of the valley; they even had several thousand Russian cavalry in reserve. The Light Brigade was vastly outnumbered.

Moreover, on each side of the valley were elevated, dug in positions containing Russian artillery and riflemen. The Light Brigade would be exposed to enemy fire from three different directions at the same time. The Russians had 20 battalions of infantry and over fifty cannons on the sides and at the end of the valley.

What's more, the Russians were fully alerted to British presence and had a clear line of sight. All British and Russian eyes saw the same sight. It was suicide to charge such a position, be it light or heavy brigade. Having seen the scene of their impending death, the regiments of British cavalry tightened their saddles and took a breath. Not one horse turned back, not one soldier wavered from the command. The Light Brigade began their mile long charge down, down into the valley of death.

It was a downward slope to the Russian position at the end of the valley. Lord Cardigan was out in front, sword held high. Suddenly a horseman veered out of the pack and angled towards Cardigan. It was Captain Nolan, waving his arm to get Cardigan's attention.

It has oft been speculated that Nolan, realizing the Light Brigade was charging the wrong position, attempted to abort the approaching tragedy. We will never know for certain, for as Captain Louis Nolan neared Cardigan the enemy opened fire. A shell knocked Nolan off his horse and to the ground, where he died instantly.

The second British casualty had "his head clean carried off by a round shot, yet for about 30 yards further the headless body kept in the saddle," a survivor recalled. Another survivor, miraculously, was Lord Cardigan, who led the charge to its final conclusion. He later told the House of Commons:

"We advanced down a gradual descent of more than three-quarters of a mile, with the batteries vomiting forth upon us shells and shot, round and grape, with one battery on our right flank and another on the left, and all the intermediate ground covered with the Russian riflemen." (See Sources for citation)

Another witness, *London Times* war correspondent William Russell, wrote:

"The whole line of the enemy belched forth, from thirty iron mouths, a flood of smoke and flame through which hissed the deadly balls, Their flight was marked by instant gaps in our ranks, the dead men and horses, by steeds flying wounded or riderless across the plain."(See sources for citation)

The first line of the Brigade was annihilated. Horses and men were splattered all over the valley. The second line of cavalry gritted their teeth, then roaring as one spurred their steeds into an even fuller gallop over their broken comrades, and straight into smoke so thick it was "like riding into the mouth of a volcano," a survivor remembered.

Viewed from behind, Russell wrote that the Brigade appeared "with a halo of flashing steel above their heads, and with a cheer which was many a noble fellow's death cry, they flew into the smoke of the batteries."

Against all odds and with miraculous resolve, not one rider turned away from the hellish fire of shell, grapeshot, canister, and rifle bullet. The second line of cavalry suffered the fate of the first. Now the third line of cavalry surged forward with a shout.

The Light Brigade finally reached the guns at the end of the valley and, with a leaping of horses, breached the enemy's position. Swords flashing, the Brigade cut and hewed their way around the artillery, causing confusion and dismay in the Russian ranks. Then they turned to the Russian cavalry and scattered them as well.

Lord Russell remembered:

"Through the clouds of smoke we could see their sabers flashing as they rode up to the guns and dashed between them, cutting down the gunners as they stood. The blaze of their steel, like an officer standing near me said, 'was like the turn of a shoal of mackerel." (That means it was bright)

Lord Cardigan was amidst the Russian batteries, and later reported:

"We entered the battery—we went through the battery—the two leading regiments cutting down a great number of the Russian gunners in their onset. In the two regiments which I had the honour to lead, every officer, with one exception, was either killed or wounded, or had his horse shot under him or injured.

"Then came the third line, which endeavored to complete the duty assigned to our brigade. ...this body succeeded in passing through the mass of Russian cavalry of—as we have since learned—5,240 strong; and having broken through that mass they ...retired in the same manner." (See Sources for citation)

The Light Brigade was forced to retreat under heavy fire. On the way back out of the valley they again encountered bitter fire from three directions before finally escaping. The entire event lasted 35 minutes.
Russell wrote:

"We saw them riding through the guns, as I have said; to our delight, we saw them returning, after breaking through a column of Russian infantry and scattering them like chaff...wounded men and dismounted troopers flying towards us told the sad tale -- demigods could not have done what they had failed to do." (See Sources for citation)

Upon regrouping, only 195 men of the original 673 were still with horses. 118 men were killed, 127 were wounded, and about 60 were taken prisoner. Over half the Brigade's horses were either killed in battle or destroyed later because of wounds.
Weeks after the battle (November 12, 1854) word reached England. Russell's account of the action was so riveting it inspired poet Alfred Tennyson to write a poem

about the event called, "The Charge of the Light Brigade." The ode was an instant classic, with the famous line "Into the valley of death rode the 600," and its outspoken finger pointing at military leadership.

It is said the Russians believed the Light Brigade to be drunk when they began their charge. War correspondent Russell concluded:"Our Light Brigade was annihilated by their own rashness, and by the brutality of a ferocious enemy." A participant in the charge called it "the most magnificent assault known in military annals and the greatest blunder known to military tactics." A French general added: "It is magnificent; but it is not war."

Here is a study in contrasts: the bravery of the Light Brigade and the stupidity and incompetence of military leadership which, unlike the charge, was not a one-time occurrence. Poor maps, poor intelligence, not knowing the strength of the enemy, and not even knowing where the enemy was, were only the beginning of sorrows.

Believing the conflict in Crimea would be over quickly, no winter clothing or even medical supplies were available to troops when winter came. Leadership had no answer to outbreaks of cholera that ended up killing more soldiers than Russian guns. By the end of the conflict British total deaths were 21,097: 2755 were killed in action; 2,019 died of wounds; 16,323 died of disease.

French losses were even more staggering. Total dead 95,000: 10,000 killed in action; 20,000 died of wounds; and 60,000 died of disease.

In England there was public outcry because the soldiers were suffering under such conditions. Dozens of nurses volunteered to go to Crimea to help the soldiers. The supervisor of the nurses was named Florence Nightingale. Under her guidance fatalities from disease sharply decreased.

In 1855 the Russian base at Sevastopol surrendered. In

1856 Russia agreed to keep its naval fleets out of the Black Sea, and the Crimean war was ended. There were 750,000 deaths in the war.

On May 14, 1927, Edwin Hughes died. He was the last survivor of the charge.

On the 150th anniversary of the Charge of the Light Brigade (2004), a commemoration was held at Balaklava, and a monument was presented to honor the 25,000 British soldiers who fought in the Crimean War.

Sources

Quotations from Lord Cardigan can be found at: https://warfarehistory.wordpress.com/2013/02/18/lord-cardigan-and-the-charge-of-the-light-brigade-balaclava-1854/

All quotations by Lord William Russell are from:

Russell, William Howard, The British Expedition to the Crimea (1858); Royle, Trevor, Crimea: the Great Crimean War, 1854-1856 (2000).

http://www.historyofwar.org/articles/wars_crimean.html, The Crimean War.

http://www.nationalarchives.gov.uk/battles/crimea/after.htm,

http://www.pinetreeweb.com/13th-balaclava2.htm,

"The Charge of the Light Brigade, 1854", EyeWitness to History, http://www.eyewitnesstohistory.com (2008).

Death And Glory:
Ascending Mount Everest

Climbers who die on the mountain are left where they perish because the effects of altitude make it nearly impossible to drag bodies away. Those ascending Everest pass through an icy graveyard littered with remnants of old tents and equipment, empty oxygen canisters, and frozen corpses." Borgna Brunner, Everest Almanac.

THERE IS AN area of the great mountain called the death zone for all who have died there. There the cold is so bitter it instantly freezes exposed flesh. Snow is frozen solid and slippery enough to send you sliding to your doom. Two hundred mile per hour jet stream winds can blow you right off the rock. You can pass out from oxygen deprivation and fall or pass out and die.

Frozen corpses in the death zone and elsewhere may rest forever on Mount Everest. It is simply too physically exhausting to move the bodies. Presently there are over 250 corpses at various points on the mountain. Frozen in time at the moment of their deaths, the bodies are referred to as "sleeping beauties."

May 29 is the anniversary of the first climbers to reach

the top of Mount Everest. In 1953 New Zealander Edmund Hilary and Sherpa Tenzing Norgay toiled up the southern face of the mountain, a shrewd route selected after careful planning. At long last Hilary set his foot on the summit. Then Sherpa Tenzing did. The two men rejoiced and hugged each other. Hilary took pictures of the view. Sherpa Tenzing waved flags from England, Nepal, and India. They buried sweets and a cross in the snow.

Hilary described the peak of Everest as "a symmetrical, beautiful snow cone summit." To avoid becoming corpses, however, Hilary and Sherpa Tenzing could only spend fifteen minutes at the top of the world. Their oxygen supply was low, and they had to descend back through the death zone, that infamous part of the earth that does not have enough oxygen to sustain human life.

Hilary and Sherpa Tenzing made it down alive, arriving at base camp looking like death warmed over. Seeing their condition, their comrades assumed they had failed to reach the summit. When they learned the happy truth there were toasts and huzzahs all around. Queen Elizabeth, quietly ignoring the fact Hilary was a mere Kiwi, knighted him immediately.

The feat of Edmund Hilary and Sherpa Tenzing was the culmination of a century of fascination over Himalayan mountains by the British government. A positive aspect of British colonialism in India was the Great Trigonometric Survey of India, its borders, and the Himalayan Mountain range. The survey was an ambitious attempt to explore and define the geography, distances, and heights of the wild lands of India, Nepal, and Tibet. When the project began in 1802 it was intended to last five years. Sixty years and seven hundred employees later, the Survey not only completely mapped out India, but it also determined with impressive accuracy the heights of the highest peaks of the

Himalayan mountains.

The highest peak was named Peak XV. As Surveyor General of India, Welsh geographer George Everest was responsible for planning and executing the rigorously scientific measurements that resulted in Peak XV being declared 29,002 feet high. So instrumental was Colonel Everest to this endeavor that his successors named Peak XV after him. Everest complained to no avail. It may have been a small victory for him that the pronunciation of Mount Everest (EV-uh-rest) is different than the actual pronunciation of his name (EEVE-wrist).

The great mountain had other, older names from its neighbors in Nepal, Tibet, and China. Tibetans called it *Chomolungma* ("Holy Mother") and built monasteries in the foothills. Chinese call it *Zhumulangma* ("Holy Mother Peak") and had explored it since the 1700's. The newest name for Everest was coined by the Nepalese government in the 1960's: *Sagarmatha* ("Goddess of the Sky"). In 1975 the Chinese surveyed Everest and amended its height to 29,029 feet. It is the highest mountain above sea level in the world, and the highest borderland: Everest's summit marks the border between Tibet (China) and Nepal.

All the early recorded climbs of Everest were done by the British. The most famous climber was George Mallory, a Cambridge graduate, star athlete, and climbing prodigy. In 1924 Mallory and his partner, Andrew "Sandy" Irvine started in Tibet and took a northern route up Everest. They left base camp on June 8, 1924, and never came back. News of their disappearance shocked Britain, who proclaimed the two climbers' national heroes in a memorial service attended by the British Parliament and the Royal Family. Over the years there was speculation as to whether Mallory had made it to the top of Everest before perishing. Was he the first human to set foot on the summit?

The British kept climbing Everest during the 1930's. There was even an attempt to fly a plane over Everest to drop a Union Jack flag on the summit. The first conqueror of Mount Everest, however, was a most unlikely one.

Edmund Hilary was a small, shy, bookish boy who grew up to be six feet five inches high, serve in the New Zealand Royal Air Force during World War II, and return home to become a beekeeper. He liked climbing mountains too, and became part of the ninth British expedition to Mount Everest. After one team failed, Hilary and Tenzing were ordered up the mountain.

All went according to plan until the two came upon a sheer forty-foot rock wall. Somehow Hilary wedged himself into and up a crack in the rock face. Tenzing followed. This part of the mountain is now referred to as "the Hilary Step." From there it was on to the summit, or in the words of Sir Edmund Hilary: "A few more whacks of the ice axe in the firm snow and we stood on top."

Hilary went on to explore the North Pole and South Pole. He became the only man to ever stand on both poles and on the top of Everest. Hilary created the Himalayan Trust foundation to develop schools and hospitals for the Sherpas, an ethnic group inhabiting the mountains of Nepal. Modest and mild-mannered, he preferred reading books at home in New Zealand to the public spotlight.

In 1999 the BBC sponsored a research expedition to find the bodies of George Mallory and his partner Irvine. At about 27,000 feet on the north side of the mountain a corpse was found, freeze-dried and mummified. The name tag on the clothing read "G. Leigh Mallory." An Anglican requiem service was performed, and the body was covered and left where it was. To this day no one knows if Mallory was the first to reach the top of Everest. Most mountaineers, however, do not consider a climb to be successful unless the climber returns to base camp alive.

Since Hilary's ascent of Everest, about 4,000 other climbers have reached the top. Climbing Everest is big business these days. It costs between $50,000 and $100,000 per individual to do it. None of it would be possible without the workhorses of Everest, the Sherpas, who go ahead of the climbers to set scaling ropes over the many difficult sections of the mountain, and position aluminum ladders over glacial crevasses.

In addition to the hundreds of corpses on Everest, there are hundreds of tons of rubbish. Nepal's government began a cleanup of Everest in 2001. In 2003 Sir Edmund commented on the recent rush to the top of Everest:

> "I find it all rather sad. I like to think of Everest as a great mountaineering challenge, and when you've got people just streaming up the mountain - well, many of them are just climbing it to get their name in the paper really. I do believe that many of the climbs on the mountain now lack that sense of success and exhilaration that we gained from going up. There was a much bigger challenge for us than there has been for later expeditions."(See Sources for citation)

In 2008 Sir Edmund Hilary died of a heart attack at his home in New Zealand. After a state funeral, his body lay in state at Holy Trinity Cathedral. Then Hilary's body was cremated, and the ashes were scattered in Auckland. Some ashes were saved and sent to a monastery in Nepal. Hilary's likeness appears on New Zealand currency and stamps.

People from all over the world come to Everest. But if anyone thinks Mount Everest has become child's play, a recent event provides a chilling counterpoint. On April

18, 2014, an avalanche on the mountain buried thirteen Sherpa guides. The lesson? You may ascend Everest, but you will not conquer it.

Update: The tragic avalanche on the Khumbu icefall of Mount Everest prompted a labor dispute between the Sherpas and the government of Nepal, which pockets millions of dollars from the Everest tourism industry every year. The Sherpas, by contrast, make $5,000 a year and have no worker's compensation, health insurance, or life insurance. Sherpas complain that every year their job becomes more and more dangerous, as inexperienced but wealthy climbers expect the Sherpas to chauffeur them up a very dangerous mountain.

Tempers ignited when the Nepalese government offered the Sherpa community a money settlement of roughly $400 for each lost life. This was received as a profound insult and the Sherpas voted to boycott the climbing season, which would effectively end the climbing season and smack everyone hard in the wallet, especially the climbers who had already paid tens of thousands of dollars in anticipation of a mountain climb. Even so, some of the climbers were outspoken supporters of the Sherpa boycott. The controversy has resulted in the government of Nepal creating a relief fund for the Sherpas

Sources

https://www.nationalgeographic.org›encyclopedia›mount-everest

https://BBC+News%2C+On+this+day+in+History%2C+May+29+1953.&atb=v310-7&ia=web

https://www.mount-everest.net Mount Everest, World's Highest Mountain https://www.newworldencyclopedia.org > entry > Mount_ Everest

https://www.National Geographic: Everest: Pictures and stories, nationalgeograhic.com

http://www.Mount Everest: History, Facts mnteverest.net/ history

Borgna, "Mortals on Mount Olympus – A history of climbing Mount Everest." Source for quotation at beginning of article.

David Fickling, *The Guardian*, March 12, 2003, "We knocked the Bastard Off," a profile of Sir Edmund Hilary.

https://mounteverest.info/how-many-dead-bodies-everest/

The Andrea Yates Murders: An Avoidable Tragedy

THERE ARE WORSE things than being crazy, but few things are worse than being crazy and drowning your five children in the family bathtub. Welcome to the world of Andrea Yates and the fateful day when religion met madness.

It was a crime that rivaled even the 9/11 tragedy for news headlines. On June 20, 2001, Andrea filled the family bathtub with cold water, and systematically drowned the five children she bore her husband, Rusty: Noah, age 7; John, age 6; Paul, age 4; Luke age 3; and little Mary, who was 6 months old. Noah was the last to die. He came into the bathroom and saw Mary floating in the tub. He ran, but mom caught him, dragged him into the bathroom, and submerged him right next to Mary. Noah fought for his life, breaking water twice. The second time he gasped, "I'm sorry Mommy." Andrea shoved him back under until he spoke no more.

It was a tragic end of a beautiful young family. Rusty and Andrea loved each other, and they loved their children. Both were sincerely religious. Both believed in having all the babies God wanted them to have (another way of saying they did not contracept). But after 3 births and one miscarriage, Andrea started unraveling. In June 1999, four months after Paul was born, Andrea began to believe the children would only be eternally saved if she killed herself. She overdosed on Trazodone, a sleeping medication, but survived.

The next month Andrea looked into the bathroom mirror and saw someone else's face, surrounded by darkness. Rusty found her with a knife against her throat. He wrestled it away from her and got Andrea hospitalized. The only medication that helped her was Haldol, an old line antipsychotic medication used to treat schizophrenia. Andrea was discharged from the hospital with a prescription for Haldol, and a warning not to have any more children.

Andrea's doctor believed she had severe post-partum depression with psychotic thinking. He also thought that having more children would cause Andrea's illness to recur or worsen. It is unusual that Andrea's doctor treated post-partum depression with an antipsychotic medication instead of an anti-depressant; but for some reason Haldol really seemed to work well for Andrea.

Andrea didn't like taking medications, and she wanted to have more babies. For a time she seemed to return to her old self, even without the medications. Andrea was a bright, pretty woman who was her high school classes' valedictorian. She was a competitive swimmer. Then she became a nurse and worked on the cancer ward for eight years. She was a gifted woman who loved helping others, loved God, and most of all, loved being a mother.

The Yates' fifth child, Mary, was born in November 2000. Three months later Andrea's father died . The hormonal changes and the death of a very close family member triggered a spin into psychosis. Andrea believed the media placed surveillance cameras in her home to document her failed attempts at motherhood. She started getting messages from the television accusing her of being a failure.

Convinced the numbers 666 were branded on her scalp, Andrea picked at her head, causing open sores and large scabs. Rusty took Andrea back to the hospital, where she was prescribed anti-depressants. They didn't help. Rusty took Andrea back to the hospital in May of 2001. Again, no help. By now Rusty and his mother were doing heavy lifting to keep the family afloat, and to monitor Andrea, whom they feared would again attempt suicide. No one - absolutely no one - ever dreamed she would harm her children.

On the fateful morning, Rusty left for work after arranging for his mother to come over to help Andrea in one hour. As Rusty drove off, Andrea immediately acted on a plan she had hatched the night before. She filled the tub with cold water and drowned the children in the one hour gap she had to herself. She wrapped each corpse in a white sheet and laid them side by side on the bed. Andrea called the police and said: "I just killed my kids." Then she called Rusty and said the same thing, adding: "I am Satan."

Andrea was convinced all her children had character defects severe enough to doom them to hell. She blamed her poor parenting for this. In order to save the children from hell she killed them in the belief they had not yet gotten bad enough for God to reject them. In Andrea's mind, it was a mercy killing.

Reaction to the Yates' murders was intense. There was an unusual amount of sympathy for Andrea, considering she murdered five children. Others thought Andrea should be shown the same compassion she showed her children, and suffer the same fate she imposed upon them.

Rusty became a lightning rod for criticism. He was portrayed as an ignorant religious red neck bent on keeping his wife pregnant and in the kitchen until she dropped. It was said he forced his family to live in a dilapidated trailer, and exposed Andrea to the religious extremism that eventually led her to murder. He was called cold, aloof, detached, even "goofy."

At her first trial in 2002, over 2,000 pages of medical testimony revealed that Rusty Yates had consistently been Andrea's only advocate in a mental health system that by turns misdiagnosed, mis-prescribed, and mistreated Andrea's illness. One of many absurdities occurred when Andrea was repeatedly forced to go chemical dependency groups, even though she abhorred alcohol and drugs and never used either. Rusty visited Andrea every day at the hospital. When she refused to eat hospital staff would call Rusty who made a special trip to get Andrea to eat. He was the only one she would take nourishment for. Andrea's inpatient psychiatrist was completely positive about Rusty's efforts to help his wife. The doctor described Andrea as "one of the sickest persons I've ever treated."

Rusty battled to get Andrea on Haldol, then advocated for it again when she was hospitalized just prior to the murders. But Andrea's psychiatrist put her on anti-depressants, which didn't touch Andrea's psychotic thinking, and titrated her off Haldol, the only medication that helped Andrea. A month later her children were dead.

The mental health system completely failed the Yates family. Her hospital psychiatrist had access to Andrea's records, so should have known that Haldol was the only medication that worked for Andrea. Yet under the hospital's watch Andrea was taken off Haldol. It is not exaggeration to say the mental health system was as responsible for the children dying as Andrea Yates.

As for the extreme living conditions and religious views Rusty allegedly forced on Andrea, the truth of the matter was that Andrea was always the more extremely religious of the two. Rusty was a committed Christian, but Andrea was more fervently emotional about their faith. The two were sincere, well meaning Protestants who took portions of the bible literally.

Their sincerity led them to follow a charismatic preacher named Michael Woroniecki. Andrea's emotional attachment to her faith made her an easy convert to Woroniecki's fiery brand of Christianity. The Yates' ended up following their leader to a trailer park. Then Rusty, a professional engineer with NASA, got fed up with the situation and moved his family away. In particular, he distanced his wife from Woroniecki's spell. It was Andrea, not Rusty, who kept in touch with the preacher after the Yates family had moved on.

Rusty and Andrea were viewed as religious extremists for not using birth control, and for home schooling their children. There are thousands, perhaps millions, of parents who travel the same road as Rusty and Andrea. Many of them succeed in having large families and protecting their children from what they consider the negative aspects of American culture: rampant materialism and consumerism, political and cultural norms antagonistic to Christianity, and the soft porn images and sensibilities so commonplace on television and the Internet.

Many of these families take heroic measures to follow what they believe to be God's will, and many of them succeed. Is it a path alien to secular sensibilities? Most definitely. Whether it is good or bad, however, is a matter of opinion. More than a few secular media pundits who ordinarily applaud the different and unusual seemed surprisingly intolerant of the Yates' Christianity.

In retrospect, homeschooling for Andrea Yates was a well intentioned but dire mistake. Mother and school master in one, she had no one to blame a child's bad behavior or bad grades on except herself. Homeschooling also increased her – and her family's - social isolation.

But it was not Christianity that killed the Yates children. It was Andrea's mental illness: a demon inside her that twisted every small episode she had with her children into an apocalyptic failure; an implacable spirit that magnified her children's flaws into unforgivable sins; and who distorted a loving God into a cruel and relentless judge whom Andrea could never please, only make amends to.

The final amends were sacrificing her children before she tainted them so badly that God sent them to hell. Rusty and Andrea made great – even heroic - sacrifices for what they believed in. The awful murders of the children tends to overshadow the successes Rusty and Andrea had for years raising their children according to their religious faith.

Rusty consistently refused to blame his wife for murdering their children, saying it was her mental illness that caused the murders. Did he miss his children? Desperately. Did he forgive Andrea? Absolutely, said Rusty, not only in 2001, but ever since.

In 2002 Andrea Yates was tried for capital murder with a possible death penalty. The prosecution's star witness was the celebrity expert psychiatrist Park Dietz. Dietz claimed Andrea was a cunning villain who deliberately copied her murders to match a *Law And Order* episode where a woman drowned her children and got away with murder by pleading the insanity defense.

So forceful was his opinion that the jury found Andrea sane and convicted her of murder. Only later was it discovered that there was no *Law And Order* episode like the one Dietz described. Here was yet another instance of the mental health system not having the slightest clue about what was wrong with Andrea. Malpractice anyone?

When Dietz's fabrication was discovered a new trial was ordered in 2006. Andrea was found to be not guilty by reason of insanity. She was sent to a mental hospital north of San Antonio, Texas, where she is likely to reside for the rest of her life. This was the sane year Rusty Yates re-married, reportedly with Andrea's blessing. On March 20, 2008, Rusty Yates became a father again when his second wife, Laura, bore a son they named Mark.

Rusty still e-mails and phones Andrea. Their relation-ship has retained a genuine, mutual fondness – and a gen-uine mutual grief - that has survived the deaths of their five children. While Rusty has forgiven Andrea, she has not forgiven herself. "She cries a lot," Rusty said. "She doesn't understand how I can forgive her." Andrea is finally on some medications that effectively treat her delusions. This raises a question. Which is more painful for Andrea Yates - reality or madness? Facing her crimes in the cold light of day, one wonders if she ever longs for the darkness of insanity to shroud the death of her family.

After the murders, Houston benefactors set up a $50,000 Yates Children Memorial Fund (YCMF) devoted to women's mental health education. In 2003 Texas lawmak-ers enacted the "Andrea Yates bill", requiring doctors to inform pregnant and post-partum women of related mental illnesses, including not just depression, but psychosis re-lated to or arising from depression.

Source

Are You There Alone? The Unspeakable Crime of Andrea Yates, by Suzanne O'Malley, Simon & Schuster, 2004.

What Sank the SS Edmund Fitzgerald?

"The sea has never been friendly to man. At most it has been the accomplice of human restlessness."
Joseph Conrad, novelist

THE LEAST FRIENDLY portion of Lake Superior is "Shipwreck Coast." Also known as "the graveyard of ships," Shipwreck Coast has a century's long record of ruining hundreds of ships and thousands of lives - especially in the month of November.

November is when polar Alberta Clipper winds blow south over the vast low-pressure areas of the largest body of fresh water in the world: the Great Lakes. The intense low pressure pulls polar winds and southern Gulf air together. The mixture is as explosive as it is unpredictable. It can create tornadoes, blizzards, Category two hurricane winds, and waves over thirty feet high. Sailors who have survived simply call it "the Witch of November."

The SS Edmund Fitzgerald

In 1958 the largest ship of its kind was built to travel the Great Lakes. It was named after the President and Chairman of the Board of Northwestern Mutual Life Insurance Company, Edmund Fitzgerald. His agency funded the construction of the SS (Steam Ship) Edmund Fitzgerald.

The Fitzgerald had a wealth of titles: Queen of the Lakes, Mighty Fitz, Big Fitz, or just plain Fitz. For seventeen years the Edmund Fitzgerald carried massive loads of iron ore from Duluth to various ports around the Great Lakes. The Fitzgerald broke numerous records – often its own - for cargo carried during a shipping season. It was the pride of Great Lakes shipping.

The Fitzgerald was as elegant as it was durable. Part of the interior of the ship featured expensive carpeting, tiled bathrooms, and leather chairs. Passenger and crew quarters enjoyed air conditioning. Other amenities included a large galley and food pantry. The freighter was almost as long as the *Titanic yet* could be maintained by less than thirty crew members, including the captain.

In 1972 Captain Ernest McSorley took the helm of the Edmund Fitzgerald. The Canadian born skipper had sailed the Great Lakes (and oceans) for more than forty years. He treated his crew as the professionals they were, and they returned his respect. His disregard of the Witch of November was less professional.

McSorley had a reputation as a "rough weather" captain. His tendency was to battle the elements, and the Edmund Fitzgerald was his ablest weapon. "Rough water didn't really scare him," noted a researcher. "McSorley believed in his boat, and he didn't like to waste time. He was famous for saying, 'We don't get paid for sitting here.'"

So it was with little anxiety that McSorley took the news of a storm coming across Lake Superior on the afternoon of November 9, 1975. He was sixty-three years old and had seen it all. He was planning to retire at the end of the shipping season, which was very near. In Superior,

Wisconsin, the Fitzgerald was loaded with over 26,000 tons of taconite pellets.

Their destination was Zug Island on the Detroit River. McSorley aimed the Fitz in a straight line towards the target and sailed away.

November 10, 1975

Soon after the Fitz left port the National Weather Service issued gale warnings for the area the Fitzgerald was sailing in. Winds stiffened. Waves grew over ten feet high. The Fitz carried on.

The next day brought worse weather. At 3:30 pm McSorley radioed Captain Jesse Cooper of the Arthur Anderson, a cargo ship sailing about fifteen miles behind the Fitzgerald:

"Anderson, this is the Fitzgerald. I have sustained some topside damage. I have a fence rail laid down, two vents lost or damaged, and a list. I'm checking down. Will you stay by me til I get to Whitefish?"

That the Fitzgerald was listing (tilting) to one side was a sign of significant structural damage. Whitefish Bay provided shelter from the storm. It was a haven for battered boats. McSorley's plan was an admission there was no more 'business as usual' for the Edmund Fitzgerald. He was seeking safe harbor.

Cooper agreed to keep the Anderson near the Fitzgerald until it reached Whitefish Bay. He asked McSorley if he had his pumps going. McSorley replied, "Yes, both of them." Somewhere between 5:30 and 6:00 pm, CST. the Fitzgerald radioed again: "I have a bad list, lost both radars, and am taking heavy seas over the deck. One of the worst seas I've ever been in." McSorley asked Cooper to help guide him to Whitefish Bay. Cooper obliged.

It got worse. By late afternoon the Anderson reported winds of 67 miles an hour and waves 25 feet high. Gusts of wind were recorded as high as 87 miles per hour. Then the Anderson was nearly sunk by rogue waves thirty-five feet high. The Witch of November had fully arrived.

Captain Cooper radioed the Fitzgerald at 7:10 pm, and asked McSorley how things were. "We are holding our own," he replied. Fifteen minutes later the SS Edmund Fitzgerald disappeared from the Anderson's radar screen.

There was no SOS signal. The Fitz simply disappeared, and to this very day no one knows exactly what happened. We are left with an abiding feeling that it wasn't supposed to end this way. The SS Edmund Fitzgerald: the mighty Fitz, the great ship elegant enough to host the rich and famous, and durable enough to break so many records hauling cargo across the Great Lakes. What caused the wreck of the Edmund Fitzgerald?

There was no one to answer the question. The twenty-nine men on the Edmund Fitzgerald, ranging in age from twenty-one to Captain McSorley's sixty-three, would never be able to explain exactly what happened. One can only imagine their last moments, when the sky and sea became a blinding blackness that surrounded them. They felt the roll and pitch of the ship, heard the groaning of metal tortured by nature. How much did they know before ship succumbed to sea, and sank slowly to the bottom of Lake Superior?

Afterward

The Anderson radioed the Coast Guard with the news and was ordered to search for the Fitz. The search continued the next day, November 11. Debris, lifeboats, and rafts were found. Several months later Navy divers found the Edmund Fitzgerald in two pieces in water 530 feet deep. The initial speculation was that the Fitz broke on the surface in the middle, where all the tons of taconite were loaded.

The wreck was investigated by the National Transportation Safety Board. The Board concluded that hatch covers on the deck of the Fitzgerald collapsed, resulting in a sudden and massive flooding of the cargo hold, which caused the ship to sink. This conclusion was unconvincing to many experienced mariners.

In 1995 a dive down to the wreck found a body wearing a life jacket, proving that at least one crew member was aware of danger. By now another theory of how the Fitz sank developed. Cooper had reported two (possibly three) rogue waves that battered the Anderson, then headed in the direction of the Fitzgerald. Known as "three sisters," the rogue waves crash onto a ship's deck in shattering succession, each wave leaving tons of water on the deck. Overloaded with taconite, with a low waterline, and with structural damage causing a serious list, how could the Fitzgerald have prevailed against such a force of nature?

The rogue wave theory is the explanation maritime experts use most often to answer the question: what sank the SS Edmund Fitzgerald?

The 1995 dive was the last legal dive allowed on the Fitzgerald. The divers claimed the 200-pound bell of the Edmund Fitzgerald. The bell was restored and today is displayed at the Great Lakes Shipwreck Museum in Michigan. Every November 10th the bell is ceremoniously rung 29 times for each crewman of the SS Edmund Fitzgerald.

Today the wreck site is classified a graveyard. Diving the wreck is forbidden so the dead can rest in peace. They are gone but not forgotten. The wreck of the Fitz has been explored in numerous books over the years. Perhaps the most enduring response to the tragedy is a ballad written in 1976 by Canadian folk singer Gordon Lightfoot. Entitled "The Wreck of the Edmund Fitzgerald," Lightfoot's lyrics are accurate and heart-rending, especially the line: "Does anyone know where the love of God goes when the waves turn the minutes to hours?"

Where indeed was the love of God on the night of November 10th? Perhaps at the cold, dark bottom of Lake Superior, patiently waiting to greet 29 valiant seamen, and take them home.

Sources

The SS Edmund Fitzgerald Online (SSEFO)

Too Deep, Too Dark, Too Cold, by Jeannine Ouellette with Jon Zurn, published in The Rake, November 2003.

Wikipedia entries for *The SS Edmund Fitzgerald, Lake Superior, Gordon Lightfoot.*

You Tube video, Gordon Lightfoot performing The Wreck of the Edmund Fitzgerald.

Double Fantasy: John Lennon and Mark Chapman

ON THE LAST day of his life John Lennon did a photo shoot for the cover of *Rolling Stone* magazine. When photographer Annie Leibovitz visited Lennon mid-afternoon on December 8, 1980, however, Lennon insisted on having his wife, Yoko Ono, in the picture. Adhering to the "*never argue with a superstar*" handbook for photojournalists, Leibovitz shot the Lennon's together. The results were remarkable.

The next cover of *Rolling Stone* featured Yoko lying flat on her back. She wore all black and her long black hair fanned out from her black clothes onto the floor. Lennon was completely naked. His left arm wrapped around Yoko's head, his lips kissed her cheek, and his torso and legs were wrapped up in an extreme fetal position. John Lennon never saw the picture.

After the photo shoot Lennon did a radio interview discussing his newly released (November 1980) album *Double Fantasy*, and the Number One single from the album, "(Just Like) Starting Over." Lennon had been out of music the last five years, fighting the US government's deportation efforts, trying to kick drugs, and raising he and Yoko's son, Sean.

Now he was back in the spotlight again. There was even talk of a world tour. It was a coming out party of sorts for John Lennon – and of course his wife, Yoko Ono, the avant-garde Japanese artist who captivated Lennon and won his heart, for better and worse.

Lennon was not an easy man to live with. He was fiercely independent, fiercely intelligent, physically violent, and drug addicted. The man who sang of peace, challenging everyone to imagine a world with no attachments and aversions, had precious little peace in his private life. He was a heroin addict for years and showered everyone with his acerbic wit and negative instant karma. In return, his post-Beatles career was savaged by critics and others with spots still tender from Lennon's barbs (like the US government).

But during late afternoon, December 8, 1980, Lennon took time to chat with fans and sign autographs outside his residence. He had lived at the Dakota for years and was used to fans hanging out at the entrance. For all his vices and defects, Lennon could also be easy going, down to earth, and kind. Although he and Yoko were running late for a recording session, Lennon took extra time to chat with as many fans as possible.

An overweight young man with glasses handed the superstar a copy of *Double Fantasy.* Lennon autographed the album cover, handed it back to the young man, and asked: "Is this all you want?" The man smiled and nodded his head. His name was Mark David Chapman. He had been waiting outside the entrance to the Dakota since morning.

A photographer named Paul Goresh took a picture of Lennon autographing Chapman's album. As the Lennon's entered their limousine Goresh prepared to leave. Chapman turned to Goresh and said, "I'd wait. You never know if you'll see him again." Paul Goresh never saw John Lennon again. Mark Chapman did.

At this point in his life Mark David Chapman was a hot mess, but he had always been a bit off. Growing up in Decatur, Georgia, he developed an inner life that featured imaginary "little people" who lived in the walls of his bedroom. He read and reread J.D. Salinger's *Catcher in the Rye,* a novel about a teenage boy with a rich, tortured inner life, and no social skills.

In high school he excelled working for the YMCA as a camp counselor. The kids affectionately nicknamed Mark "Nemo." The other activity Chapman excelled in was dropping LSD as often as he could. A friend said Chapman did LSD hundreds of times, along with heroin, mescaline, and barbiturates.

Taking LSD was a religious experience for Chapman. He loved listening to the Beatles – especially John Lennon - while he was high. They were Mark's favorite group until his junior year in high school when he quit drugs and became a born-again Christian. He witnessed publicly about his faith and alienated some friends. Chapman turned hardest against the Beatles – John Lennon in particular.

Lennon was famous for his quote that the Beatles were more popular than Jesus. Many, if not most, misunderstood his point which was that Beatles fans lacked a sense of proportion about what was truly important in life. Lennon was accused of posturing as a deity. In the south, where Chapman grew up, there were groups that burned Beatles records, and radio stations that refused to play Beatles music. When the lads from Liverpool toured America's southland in 1966, the booing of crowds was punctuated by the throwing of garbage and firecrackers at the stage. The Beatles never toured the south again.

It is one thing to take issue with John Lennon's statement about God and the Beatles. It is quite another to kill him for it. But before Chapman began stalking Lennon, he tried to kill himself – more than once. Mark's life wasn't turning out the way he wanted it to. The girl he loved ended their relationship because Mark wasn't Christian enough for her. He became depressed and felt like a failure. He moved to Hawaii and tried to kill himself twice. Both attempts failed.

Chapman seemed to recover. He married in 1979, got a job as a security guard, and was trained to shoot a pistol. Chapman became an excellent marksman. Then he relapsed into depression again and quit his job in October 1980. He sold some artwork to buy a .38-caliber revolver (but no bullets). He also began drinking, doing cocaine, and talking to the imaginary "little people" again.

Chapman's longtime obsession with J.D. Salinger's book *Catcher in the Rye* moved to the front burner. Chapman had an absolute identification with protagonist Holden Caulfield. He called himself Holden Caulfield and signed notes and letters with Caulfield's name. Like Caulfield, Mark David Chapman became obsessed with phoniness. He decided the biggest phony in the world was John Lennon: a man who preached non-materialism, peace, and love, yet lived in luxury. For this, Chapman decided, John Lennon must die.

Chapman flew to New York City in October 1980 to find Lennon. What he found instead was a law in New York prohibiting him from buying bullets. Chapman flew down to Atlanta to get bullets from an unwitting friend. The bullets were hollow point: the hollowed-out tip causes the bullet to expand on impact, maximizing tissue and organ damage. Chapman flew back to New York and got muddled again: he couldn't decide whether to kill himself by jumping off the Statue of Liberty or to kill John Lennon instead. He split the difference and flew back to Hawaii.

Back home, Chapman changed his mind again and told his wife he was going to kill John Lennon. He showed her his gun and the bullets. She didn't call the police. Why? Perhaps she sought to protect her husband, or perhaps she was in sheer disbelief that Mark David Chapman could do anything on that large of a scale. The couple made an appointment for Mark to see a psychologist, but he flew back to New York before the appointment.

Arriving in New York on December 6, 1980, Chapman got a room at the YMCA. Two days later he was outside the Dakota, a nineteenth-century luxury residence inhabited by millionaires and celebrities. Chapman saw Gilda Radner, Lauren Bacall, Paul Simon, and Mia Farrow enter and leave the building. Apartments at the Dakota go for 4 to 20 million dollars. Chapman was appalled that the man who wrote "Imagine no possessions" lived so expensively.

But when he came face to face with Lennon outside the Dakota, he was speechless. Lennon seemed like a normal, even a nice man – not the monster of phoniness Chapman imagined him to be. Chapman had a copy of *Double Fantasy* with him to look like a fan. Lennon stopped and signed it. Then, according to Chapman, Lennon:

> "looked at me very earnestly and very sincerely in my eyes and started to hand me back the album— He said, "Is that what you wanted? Is that all you want?" And I said, "Yeah, thanks. Thanks a lot." I was just overwhelmed by his sincerity. I had expected a brush-off, but it was just the opposite.... I was on cloud nine. And there was a little bit of me going, "Why didn't you shoot him?" And I said, "I can't shoot him like this...." I wanted to get the autograph (See Sources for citation)."

Lennon left Chapman with his autographed record and entered a limousine with Yoko. It was 5:45 pm. They were driven to the Record Plant Studio to record a song Yoko wrote called "Walking on Thin Ice." Later Chapman said he prayed for the strength to not kill Lennon. When it came right down to it, however, Chapman said, "It was almost as if I was on some kind of special mission that I could not avoid." At 10:50 pm he was back outside the Dakota, waiting.

Lennon's limousine pulled up in front of the building. It happened that Yoko wanted to go to a restaurant after recording, but John wanted to be home in time to say goodnight to his son before going out to eat. John and Yoko walked towards the entrance. Lennon was holding a cassette tape of Ono's "Walking on Thin Ice."

Mark David Chapman stood in the shadows near the archway. Lennon looked at him as he passed by. Later Chapman recalled:

> "He walked past me, and then I heard [a voice] in my head say 'Do it do it do it' over and over again, just like that. 'Do it do it do it do it do it....' He walked a few feet. I turned, pulled the gun out of my pocket.... I don't remember aiming. I must have, but I don't remember drawing a bead.... I just pulled the trigger steady five times...

> "I remember thinking, 'The bullets are working.' I thought the humidity in the plane might have gotten to them. I think I felt a little regret that they were working, but I'm not sure. I just remember thinking, 'The bullets are working.(See Sources for citation)'

Chapman had assumed a shooting position and fired five shots in quick succession. The first went through a window. The other four bullets went into John Lennon's body. Lennon staggered and fell. Blood covered the sidewalk. Yoko screamed and held him.

The doorman disarmed Chapman and shouted at him:

"Do you know what you've just done?" "Yes," Chapman replied in an even voice, "I've just shot John Lennon." Police arrived within minutes of the shooting to find the shooter sitting on the sidewalk, holding a paperback copy of *The Catcher in the Rye.*

A policeman hauled Lennon's body over his shoulder and took him to nearby Roosevelt Hospital. Upon arrival Lennon had no blood pressure, no pulse. Dr. Stephan Lynn recalled:

"I actually held his heart in my hand as the nurses rapidly transfused blood. I tried to massage the heart as we put blood into his body. We knew that there was no way that we could restore circulation, there was no way that we could repair the massive injury to all of the blood vessels in the body. (See Sources for citation)."

Lennon was dead on arrival. His sobbing wife was given John's wedding ring and led away. The outpouring of grief was worldwide. Several Beatles fans committed suicide. On December 14 Ono requested a 10-minute silent vigil. Millions around the world participated. Lennon's body was cremated. There was no funeral service.

Mark David Chapman's lawyers wanted to make an insanity plea. Chapman disagreed and pled guilty to second-degree murder. He is still in prison. Every two years he comes up for parole, and each time he is denied. In 2012 Chapman told the board: "I felt that by killing John Lennon I would become somebody and instead of that I became a murderer and murderers are not somebodies (See Sources for citation)."

Some years before he was killed John Lennon declared:

"Neither of us [Yoko or I] want to make the mistake that Gandhi and Martin Luther King did, which is get killed one way or the other. Because people only like dead saints, and I refuse to be a saint or a martyr (See Sources for citation)."

What a nice fantasy that is – that we can pick the way we die. Even when we think we know what we are doing, life – in the form of other people – disrupts our best-laid plans. John Lennon refused the path of a martyr or a saint, but he had no control over the world's reaction to his death; like Gandhi, Lennon became a secular saint. Mark Chapman expected fame from his actions and got the kind of fame he ended up renouncing. Two very different lives, two very different fantasies – John Lennon's and Mark David Chapman's – became intertwined, and the result shook the world.

Sources

Jones, Jack (1992). *Let Me Take You Down: Inside the Mind of Mark David Chapman, the Man Who Killed John*. Lennon, Villard Books.

New York Daily News, Mark Chapman Tells His Version of the John Lennon Slaying, Tuesday August 19, 2008.

http://john-lennon.net/whoauthorizedtheassassinationof-johnlennon.html. This is the source for Chapman's quote of "Do it, do it, do it...

Mark Chapman: The Assassination of John Lennon, from Crime and Investigation.co.uk/crime-files. This is the source for Lennon's remarks about not wanting to be a saint.

Descent into Madness, James R. Gaines, *The Life and Crime of Mark David Chapman*.

https://www.bbc.com/news/entertainment-arts-11926898, for the quotation of Dr. Lynn holding John Lennon's heart in his hands.

Daily Mail UK, Mark David Chapman's Chilling Letters.

Undefeated: Rocky Marciano

WHICH HEAVYWEIGHT BOXING champion in the last century knelt on his knees to pray to St. Anthony before his first title fight, read *The Confessions of St. Augustine* before defending his title, and said: "The biggest thrill I could think of would be an audience with the pope?"

The answer: Rocky Marciano, heavyweight boxing champion from 1952 to 1956, when at age thirty-three he retired with a perfect record (49-0, with 43 knockouts) in the ring. Equally unique, Marciano never came out of retirement to challenge subsequent champions, a temptation very few ex-champions have overcome, much less succeeded at.

He was born Rocco Francis Marchegiano (Mark a-*jahn*-o) on September 1, 1923, the second son (the first died shortly after childbirth) of Pierino and Lena Marchegiano, first-generation Italian immigrants who came to America after the first World War. Pierino's exposure to mustard gas during combat changed his life, but not his toughness. Asked about his reaction when flying shrapnel hit his jaw and snapped off some teeth, Pierino replied, "I just spit them out and kept coming."

He and Lena settled in Brockton, a small city twenty

miles south of Boston. Until Rocco put Brockton on the national map, his hometown was best known for its shoe factories. Rocco inherited his father's toughness, for he survived a deadly bout of pneumonia when he was two. Lena's doctor said she could have no more children; this put a fine edge on her concern for Rocco's health.

Lena prayed to St. Anthony for her son's recovery, promising to give up her diamond engagement ring if Rocco recovered. She and her friends prayed the Rosary at the child's bedside and waited. At the time many children died of pneumonia, but Rocco eventually recovered, and Lena kept her promise.

The doctor was wrong. The Marchegiano's had five more children after Rocco: Alice, Connie, Elizabeth, Louis, and Peter. They all lived in a two-bedroom apartment. Rocco slept in the living room with the windows open, even in the winter, as if in defiance of his bout with pneumonia.

His upbringing was steeped in Italian customs and traditions. His parents loved opera, ate Italian food, and had wine with dinner. As a boy Rocco was preoccupied with his physical condition. When he wasn't playing sports he was running and exercising.

After serving as a GI in World War II, Rocco played minor league baseball. At the time boxing was a diversion, a way to make a few bucks to help out his family. Then he was cut from the Chicago Cubs farm system. Rocco was in his twenties, when most fighters hit their peak. He had no boxing skills. He was awkward in the ring. He was undersized for a heavyweight. Rocco's biggest limitation was arms so short they were almost stubby. It is difficult to win a fight when you can't reach your opponent. On those occasions Rocco reached opponents with his right hand they fell down and didn't get up.

Marchegiano went to New York and met Al Weill, a boxing

manager who tried to Americanize his name. Rocco refused but eventually he tired of having his name misspelled and mispronounced, and allowed his name to be shortened to Rocky Marciano. Rocky slowly became a better boxer, but it was his punching power that kept him undefeated. He knocked out nine of his early opponents in the first round. Several opponents quit boxing after being knocked out by Marciano. Once he hit a man so hard he almost killed him. Marciano spent hours at his opponent's hospital bed, and in church praying for the man's life. He said if the man died he would quit fighting. The man recovered but never fought again.

(An experiment was performed on Rocky's punching power. The 1963 issue of *Boxing Illustrated* claimed: "Marciano's knockout blow packs more explosive energy than an armour-piercing bullet and represents as much energy as would be required to spot lift 1000 pounds one foot off the ground." Although this sort of 'science' was probably conducted by Marciano fans, it is undeniably true Rocky hit *really* hard.)

After knocking out an old Joe Louis, Rocky got a title shot. The champion was Jersey Joe Walcott, a ring veteran most experts picked to beat Marciano easily. Before the fight Marciano met with a priest, who after their meeting said: "That boy is no ordinary prizefighter, he is one of the most dignified, straightforward people I have ever met in my life. The people of the world should be informed of this boy's character and personality."

Marciano's character was on display in his first fight with Walcott, which was a classic. Walcott's experience kept Marciano off-balance and sometimes made him look ridiculous. Rocky kept coming, even after Walcott knocked him down, closed his left eye, and opened cuts on his face that required fourteen stitches to close.

Far behind on points late in the fight, Rocky needed a knockout to win. He backed Walcott into the ropes. Walcott bounced off and threw a hard left hand. Marciano stepped inside and beat Walcott to the punch with a short right hand that traveled maybe eight inches. It hit Walcott's jaw with the sound of a baseball bat. Walcott collapsed to the canvas and was counted out. Rocky Marciano was champion.

Marciano's determination in the Walcott fight showed the world the new champion's character and personality. Although he enjoyed being champion, Marciano remained unchanged. The nicest thing about being champ, he said, "is that people like you." Everyone but boxing experts, who found Rocky's style too crude to suffer. Rocky was a brawler. He hit his opponents on the break, after the bell, and below the belt. Rocky always apologized, but the fouling continued.

As he continued to successfully defend his title, Marciano gradually drew respect from critics. He would never be a classic boxer, but he worked unceasingly at improving his craft, and trained relentlessly. One sportswriter said Marciano brought the "austere, sackcloth-and -ashes approach of a monk" to his training. The famous sportswriter Jimmy Cannon observed that Marciano trained "like a man practicing a holy ritual." Before fights he would slip away to a church or chapel to pray. Sometimes he would cover his chin and hands with St. Jude's oil while in his corner waiting for the start of a fight.

Rocky was an old-school Catholic. He would interrupt his training schedule to attend Mass. Once, as a joke, the reigning sex symbol, Jayne Mansfield, was smuggled into a room where Marciano sat, alone. A few minutes later she came out complaining: "What is he, crazy? He didn't want anything to do with me." Marciano seemed more comfortable in the company of clergy than actresses. He golfed with priests, helped promote parish functions, even lunched with Cardinal Spellman. *Life* magazine called him "pure of speech" and "a clean living boy." He was elsewhere described as "astonishingly innocent," and "totally without deception, totally without guile." He didn't drink or smoke; in fact, when a host at a party for Marciano in Brockton offered the champ a drink, Rocky replied, "If you don't mind, I'll take an apple."

Not that there is anything particularly Catholic about being a teetotaler. It's just that Marciano, though intelligent, was a very simple man who never forgot where he came from. Even as champion he came to the ring in a robe bearing the colors of Brockton High School (even though he dropped out in the tenth grade). And Brockton loved him right back, at least in part because many of them became rich betting on Rocky's fights.

While sportswriters criticized Marciano's boxing shortcomings, no one criticized his character, as the following quotes show:

> Marciano was "a kind and decent man.", He was "inherently a decent, righteous and truly wonderful guy...His innate decency and wholesomeness shine through in a dedicated glow." Or: "We never cease to be amazed at the humility of Rocky Marciano...he treats everyone if they were the celebrity and he the awed little guy." Another writer called him "probably the humblest of heavyweight champions." Said another: "He reminds you of a great, friendly collie ... with the grin of a shy fellow happy to be recognized, at last, as a member of the gang in good standing." He was "the gentlest athlete I have ever known," and again: "a man of simplicity and sincerity."

Perhaps it was his simplicity that allowed him to retire after beating everyone worth fighting. Yet his retirement years revealed a man who seemed simple, but often was not.

Rocky ran from an early age. His fanaticism about physical conditioning, along with his determination and punching power, led to an unequalled record for a heavyweight champion: forty-nine professional wins, no defeats, forty-three victories by knockout. It was an incredible run. After the Rock retired he kept running.

Outwardly Marciano's life after boxing was quite successful – unlike many fighters, he kept his money and his wits. He retained his public life, crisscrossing across the country to give speeches, participate in benefits, and conduct business. He was invited to the White House to meet the President. He even had a role in a movie. He was famous, successful, and well thought of.

He rarely saw his wife and children; or his parents, brothers, and sisters. His marriage was strained. His wife, Barbara, was unable to have the large family Rocky wanted. They had one daughter, but Barbara miscarried when Rocky was away, and wasn't able to have any more children, although the two did adopt a boy (Rocky Jr.). Barbara missed Rocky, and sometimes drank too much. She smoked too, and developed a glandular problem. Rocky seemed too busy to be home.

Maybe Rocky ran to avoid an estranged relationship with Barbara. Or the estrangement may have developed over Rocky's running, which may have sprung from a preoccupation with money. His friends said the only thing Rocky was afraid of was being poor. Yet even after he had enough money Rocky went after more. He didn't trust lawyers or accountants, and preferred to deal in cash. Rocky didn't trust banks, either, so he hid his cash: in the ground, inside toilet tanks, in light fixtures. He even used a coat hanger to stuff money inside curtain rods.

Rocky was generous with people who were down and out, often giving them unsecured loans that were rarely paid back. Rocky never wrote anything down, he tried to keep track of his loans in his head, and sometimes forgot who owed him, and how much. Yet he used a wire to try to get coins back he used to make telephone calls. And he could be incredibly tight with a buck. He usually didn't pay anything for his cross-country trips: no plane fare, hotel fare, or meals. He made sure the people who invited him paid for everything.

Rocky's last big payday was a computerized fight with Muhammed Ali in 1969. Rocky hadn't fought or trained for fourteen years. Ali was in retirement too, after having his title stripped for refusing the draft. Marciano went back into training and bought a toupee. Then Rocky and Ali sparred 70 rounds for the camera, simulating different endings to the fight. Ali later said that Marciano punched so hard he was sore for days after. The sparring film would be spliced together to match the computer outcome of the fight – a closely guarded secret that would not be revealed until "The Superfight" aired in theaters.

On August 31, 1969, Marciano planned to interrupt his business circuit and fly back to Florida to celebrate his forty-sixth birthday with his family. At the last minute Rocky decided to squeeze in an appearance at a steakhouse in Des Moines, Iowa. There would be good food, a nice check for a few words, and still enough time to fly back for his birthday. He boarded a small, single-engine Cessna. There was bad weather and the plane ran low on gas. The pilot landed the plane in a field in Newton, Iowa, and rammed into a lone tree in the middle of the field. The pilot and his two passengers were instantly killed. Marciano's body was found pinned beneath the wreckage. An obituary in his home state of Massachusetts read:

"In this age of the anti-hero and the non-hero, Rocky Marciano was the hero with whom the mass of Americans could readily identify, the hero who surmounted all difficulties by dint of hard work, dedication and perseverance. He was a near-classic example of the triumph of classic virtues (*Boston Herald Traveler*, September, 1969)."

An investigation into the crash of the Cessna in Newton Iowa cited pilot inexperience as the cause of the crash. The pilot had not flown at night before, became confused by the bad weather, and attempted to land in a field rather than the Newton airport.

Marciano died without a will. Although he left thousands (some claim hundreds of thousands) of dollars stashed away or buried underground, none of it was found to aid Barbara and the children, who were impoverished after Rocky's death.

Five months after Marciano's death "The Superfight" debuted in theaters. The computer's result: Marciano knocked out Ali in the thirteenth round. Ali complained about his 'loss', alleging the computer was made in Alabama.

In 1976 Sylvester Stallone began his "Rocky" franchise. Stallone credited Chuck Wepner's losing effort in a fight with Muhammed Ali as the inspiration for the film, yet the similarities of Rocky Balboa to Rocky Marciano are numerous and obvious.

Sources

Everett M. Skehan, *Rocky Marciano, Biography of a First Son*, Houghton Mifflin Company, Boston, 1977.

Russell Sullivan, *Rocky Marciano, The Rock of His Times*, 2002, University of Illinois Press, Urbana and Chicago.

Remembering The Alamo

TODAY SAN ANTONIO Texas is best known for its professional basketball team, the Spurs. The city's more enduring fame reaches back to 1836, when San Antonio hosted a battle that assumed mythic proportions in American history: the siege of the Alamo. What happened there?

If it were claimed American history is a century's long war over land, Texas could be offered as proof. Yet way before America and Mexico fought over Texas, Spanish missionaries claimed the land of Texas for Spain against the challenges of France and England.

Spanish Franciscans visited Texas on June 13 1691 - the feast day of fellow Franciscan Saint Anthony of Padua. Anthony's fellow Franciscans took the coincidence as a good omen. They called the area San Antonio and started civilizing it. A mission and chapel were built for the Christianizing of the local Payaya Indians. The chapel complex was originally called Mission de San Antonio de Valero.

To protect missionary efforts the Spanish added a fort and jail, called Presidio San Antonio de Bexar. The military presence meant to discourage Indian raids, intrusions by the French from nearby New Orleans, and occasional English explorers. The fort and mission were the beginnings of today's San Antonio.

By the end of the eighteenth-century Spanish missionary

efforts waned and the mission was abandoned. In the nine-teenth century Mexico won independence from Spain. Now Mexican troops occupied the Mission de San Antonio de Valero, which they renamed "Alamo" (literally "big pop-lar") either after a nearby grove of trees, or because the Mexican cavalry unit based at the mission hailed from the Mexican town Alamo de Parras.

The Mexican troops were kept busy fending off raids by the Comanche. The Mexican government began offering land to encourage immigration to Mexican Texas, in the belief that more settlements would deter Comanche raid-ers. The price tag for the land was the requirement that immigrants learn Spanish and turn Catholic.

The land offer was attractive. Between 1825 and 1834 approximately 30,000 Americans and other Europeans moved to Mexican Texas. Most had no intention of learn-ing Spanish, turning Catholic, or even becoming religious. Some Americans brought slaves with them, another viola-tion of Mexican law. In plain words most American immi-grants to Mexican Texas were squatters.

In 1830 Mexico passed a law prohibiting immigration from the United States. The new law was difficult to en-force. So was a new system of taxation Mexico tried to im-pose on their unruly immigrants. In 1832 there was armed conflict between the immigrants and Mexican troops at Anahuac. A key figure in the fight was William Travis.

Travis left his pregnant wife to move to Mexican Texas after it was illegal to do so. He set up a law practice at Anahuac, a port town at Galveston Bay, and was a key agitator against Mexican authority in the region. Travis' first cause was far from glorious: he led a rebellion against Mexican authorities who would not return runaway slaves to their American owners.

American revolt against Mexican rule in Texas spread

quickly. American immigrants started their own provisional government but there was so much quarreling between themselves they couldn't even govern their own sessions, much less provide guidance for their fledgling republic. In December 1835 the Mexican garrison at the Alamo surrendered to the American Texan army besieging it. Travis mustered up some volunteers and settled into the Alamo. It was there he met James Bowie.

One of the more notable of an ample cast of Alamo characters was the Scotch-English James Bowie. Bowie's parents met during the American Revolution. Jim's mother tended his father's battle wounds, married him, and together they had ten children – Jim was ninth.

The Bowie's were a frontier family. The children cleared the land, planted crops, and helped run the farm. At night they learned to read and write in English by candlelight. Jim also became fluent in Spanish and French. His reputation for fearlessness began at a young age when he roped alligators. Young Bowie was adept with weapons as well as rope. It was his skill with a knife that brought him international fame.

The incident is known as the Sandbar Fight. Bowie was at a duel between two other men on a sandbar outside of Natchez, Mississippi. His arch-enemy, Sheriff Norris Wright, was in the group supporting the opposing duelist. The two duelists shot at each other, missed, then shook hands and left the sandbar. Someone from the opposing group shot Bowie in the hip and knocked him down. Bowie got up, pulled out a large knife and charged the shooter.

The shooter hit Bowie on the head with his pistol hard enough to shatter the pistol. Bowie went down again. His enemy, Norris Wright, pulled out his sword cane and stabbed Bowie in the chest. Bowie lay on the ground in apparent death throes. Wright put his foot on Bowie's chest to pull his blade out. Grabbing Wright with his free hand, Bowie used his other hand to plunge his large knife into Wright's lower torso and rip the blade all the way up to Wright's heart. The disemboweled Wright died on the spot. Bowie got up with Wright's sword cane sticking out of his chest. He was shot again and stabbed again by his enemies before they finally retreated, leaving Bowie the unlikely winner of the fight.

The doctor tending to Bowie's many injuries expressed amazement he survived the attack. Indeed, he is one of a select few who brought a knife to a gunfight and won. Newspapers described the fight in detail, focusing on Bowie's prowess with his new, large knife. It came to be known as the "Bowie Knife" (or Arkansas Toothpick). The blade was nine inches long and an inch and a half wide.

The thirty-one-year-old Bowie was one of the few American immigrants who followed Mexican law. When he moved to Mexican Texas he became a Mexican citizen and was baptized into the Catholic Church in San Antonio. Then he sent his wife and children away to Monclova to protect them from a cholera epidemic. But in November 1835 the epidemic changed direction and struck Monclova. Bowie's entire family perished.

Bowie never recovered from the tragedy. He drank more and his health failed. Despite these deficits he remained a natural leader, and came to the Alamo with a larger group of volunteers than Travis. Bowie was voted the leader of the garrison, a result Travis seethed over. Texan general Sam Houston wanted Bowie to destroy the Alamo. Bowie insisted on shoring up the defenses and giving the approaching Mexican army a fight. Perhaps at this point in his life he had a death wish.

Mexican President Antonio Lopez de Santa Anna was a habitual gambler who won and lost fortunes in his lifetime – sometimes he even used his own money. His political fortunes mirrored his gambling career. He was kicked out of office more than any leader in Mexican history. After Santa Anna was gone things got worse and everyone forgot how much they hated him. Santa Anna came back to rule his nation until loathing replaced need and he was thrown out again.

Santa Anna was also a military general, a *caudillo* as they are called in Mexico. *Caudillos* are ruthless warriors who give no quarter and take no prisoners. Santa Anna personally led a large Mexican force to San Antonio to destroy the Texan rebellion. To swell the ranks he emptied prisons and coerced hundreds of otherwise idle Mexican men (and teenagers) to "enlist." As Santa Anna approached the Alamo volunteers arrived from Tennessee led by David Crockett.

Crockett was a frontiersman, a storyteller, and a national politician who bounced in and out of office almost as much as Santa Anna. He voted with his heart more than his head, particularly with his principled, outspoken opposition to the brutal Indian Removal Act:

> "I believed it was a wicked, unjust measure (declared Crockett) ... I voted against this Indian bill, and my conscience yet tells me that I gave a good honest vote, and one that I believe will not make me ashamed in the day of judgment."

The Indian Removal Act barely passed into law. In addition to Crockett, future president Abraham Lincoln voted against the bill, as did a solid block of Christian senators and Congressmen. Crockett wasn't a Christian. He was a freemason and a political maverick who once introduced a bill to shut down West Point Military Academy. Crockett opposed the public subsidizing of "the sons of rich men" as wasteful.

By the end of his last term Crockett had done enough to seriously annoy almost everyone. When Tennessee voters voted him out of office once more in August of 1835, David famously exclaimed: "I told the people of my district that they might go to hell, and I would go to Texas."

In fact, Congressman Crockett had been planning the move for over a year. He foresaw opportunities for land and wealth in the wake of the imminent revolution in Mexican Texas, and a welcome distance from national politics. One of the loose ends he wrapped up before leaving town was an east coast tour to promote his newly published autobiography, *A Narrative of the Life of David Crockett, Written by Himself*.

His daughter Matilda had a clear memory of her father wearing a coonskin cap and carrying a shiny new rifle. He promised his family they would all join him shortly in Texas. Crockett arrived at the Alamo with thirty Tennessee sharpshooters in February 1836. He was almost fifty years old.

Scouts monitored the approach of Santa Anna's army. Inside the Alamo, defenses were strengthened. Appeals were sent far and wide for supplies, ammunition, and volunteers. There was little response. By the time Santa Anna arrived in San Antonio with somewhere between 1,500 and 4,000 men, the Alamo defenders numbered between 150 and 189 men, not counting families, slaves, and other non-combatants.

The siege of the Alamo began on February 24. A red flag flew over the Mexican line, symbolizing no quarter. Bowie sent out an emissary to request an honorable surrender for the Alamo defenders. Santa Anna flatly rejected the offer. The Alamo defenders did not know that Santa Anna enacted a law classifying "foreigners" in Texas as "pirates." The new law prohibited the taking of prisoners, and mandated the immediate execution of said "pirates."

As the siege continued Jim Bowie fell seriously ill and was bedridden for the rest of his life. The twenty-six-year-old

Travis assumed command and rose to the occasion. For the next eleven days the Texans dodged hundreds of Mexican cannon balls. The bombardment continued at night, intentionally interfering with the Texan's sleep.

On March 3 one thousand Mexican reinforcements arrived, swelling the number of Mexican troops to several thousand. The weather turned bitterly cold. Most soldiers on both sides suffered for want of warm clothing. On the frosty early morning of March 6 the bombardment stopped. Just after the Texans fell asleep Mexican troops stormed the Alamo.

Travis called the men to their stations and leapt upon a catwalk to shoot down at Mexicans who had reached the outer wall and were waiting for the ladders to catch up to them. He caught a bullet through the head and died instantly, one of the first Texan casualties of the siege. His comrades drove the Mexicans away from the walls with volleys of rifle fire. The first charge was repulsed.

The second attack began minutes later. This time Mexican soldiers recognized weak spots all around the Alamo complex and began concentrating their numbers there. The Texans fired grapeshot through their cannons at the masses of Mexican troops wedged together. Imagine the contents of a hardware store flying at you at point-blank range. The second Mexican assault failed.

Over the years the Alamo was fortified to resist Comanche charges, but it was hopeless against a modern army with artillery. There was just too much area to guard, and the defenses were very weak in several spots all around the compound. Santa Anna called it "an irregular fortification hardly worthy of the name" and he was right. There weren't enough defenders to adequately cover all the weak spots. As the sun rose on March 6 the Mexican army stormed the Alamo for the third and final time.

All the weak spots were exploited simultaneously and

Mexicans poured into the complex from all directions. Fighting was so intense there was no time to reload after shooting. Rifles were used as clubs. Knives were pulled, and desperate hand to hand combat ensued. Men punched, kicked, and clawed each other in the cold, smoky morning.

The outnumbered defenders retreated to the fortified barracks next to the chapel. Crockett and his Tennesseans were defending the Palisade. They were too far away from the barracks and got caught in the middle of the compound. The Mexicans fired a volley at the exposed defenders, then charged with bayonets. The survivors stumbled into the barracks.

In their retreat Texan defenders neglected disabling their own cannons. Now the Mexicans turned the Alamo's cannons against the barracks room. A cannon blast blew open the door. Then there was a rifle volley into the darkness followed by a bayonet charge. Jim Bowie's sick bed became his deathbed. As the enemy charged into his room Bowie fired both his pistols, then grabbed his knife and slashed away until he was bayoneted to death.

Crockett's manner of death remains controversial. Some historians say he surrendered and was executed by Santa Anna. Others believe Crockett died in the middle of the compound as he and his men sprinted towards the barracks. No one actually saw him die, although his body was recognized on the ground in the compound. The legend of Crockett going down using his rifle as a club is possible.

By 6:30 am all the Texans were dead. Mexican casualties were 600 dead or wounded. Whatever one thinks of the Texans and their cause, their enemies paid dearly for each life they took.

Mexican soldiers roamed the compound, bayoneting and shooting any body that moved. Blood lust ran so high that less experienced Mexicans repeatedly shot and stabbed corpses, and even shot at each other. Then the defender's bodies were stacked in piles and burned, the ashes left to fall where they might.

Santa Anna began calling himself "the Napoleon of the West" and threatened to march his army to Washington. He fell a few thousand miles short of his goal. While taking a siesta at San Jacinto, Santa Anna's army was attacked and routed by General Sam Houston. The battle cry of the American army was "Remember the Alamo!"

As part of the surrender terms the Mexican army agreed to leave Mexican Texas and not come back. Santa Anna returned to Mexico in disgrace, and the dysfunctional republican government of Texas gained some breathing room to overcome its growing pains.

Mexican Texas was annexed by the United States government in 1845. This led to the American-Mexican war of 1846-1848, which was won by the United States. The Alamo itself was purchased by the state of Texas in 1883, and has been preserved by The Daughters of the Republic of Texas. It is estimated that 2.5 million tourists visit the Alamo annually.

Sources

http://www.thealamo.org,The Alamo.

http://www.history.com, The Alamo: Articles and Videos,

http://www.tamu.edu, Biography of William Travis, Texas A & M University,

http://www.heartofsanantonio.com/alamo/index.html, The Alamo: Shrine of Texas Liberty

http://www.tshaonline.org, James Bowie, Texas State Historical Association,

http://www.biography.com, David Crockett.

The Friendship of JRR Tolkien and CS Lewis, And the Creation of Middle Earth And Narnia

JRR TOLKIEN AND C.S. Lewis met in 1926 when Tolkien was Professor of Anglo-Saxon at Oxford University. As part of his reform of Oxford's language syllabus, Tolkien founded a club among the Oxford dons to popularize Old Icelandic (or Old Norse) literature. Tolkien's club was called *Kolbitar,* Icelandic for "coal biters," a term for "men who lounge so close to the fire in winter that they bite the coal."[1]

The focus of the group was reading and translating the Norse myths and legends contained in the *Edda*. The group relied on Tolkien's fluency in Old Icelandic. One group member fully shared Tolkien's passion for myth, legend, and "Northernness." His name was Clive Staples (C.S., or Jack) Lewis.[2]

After being wounded by a shell in the Great War, Lewis returned to his undergraduate studies at Oxford, specializing in English literature and philosophy. The school had "a prevailing tone of skepticism which Lewis gladly adopted."[3] He prided himself on being coldly rational and formidable in debate. In Lewis' eyes Tolkien was "a pale, fluent little chap." He wrote in his diary: "No harm in him (Tolkien), only needs a smack or two."[4]

Later Lewis said his friendship with Tolkien "marked the breakdown of two old prejudices...I had been warned never to trust a Papist, and never to trust a philologist. Tolkien was both."[5] Like Tolkien, Lewis was passionate about myth and legend. Unlike Tolkien, Lewis, the son of an Ulster Protestant, rejected Christianity altogether.

"I believe in no religion," he told a friend. "There is absolutely no proof for any of them, and from a philosophical standpoint Christianity is not even the best. All religions, that is, all mythologies to give them their proper name, are merely man's own invention." Lewis wrote poems "picturing God as a brutish force whose hatred has scarred men's lives."[6]

Conversion of C.S. Lewis

Tolkien and Lewis' relationship started from their common interest in mythology. Tolkien shared his expertise in languages with Lewis, who became Tolkien's willing student in translating the Norse myths Lewis had loved as a youngster. Tolkien rekindled a passion for Northern mythology Lewis had dismissed upon coming to Oxford. The next development was Lewis slowly edging back to the Christianity of his boyhood.

Tolkien had a part to play in this development as well. It was not a happy time for C.S. Lewis. He described himself as "kicking, struggling, resentful, and darting his eyes in every direction for a chance to escape." At long last, in 1929, Lewis described his conversion:

> "You must picture me alone in that room in Magdalen, night after night, feeling, whenever my mind lifted

even for a second from my work, the steady, unrelenting approach of Him whom I so earnestly desired not to meet. That which I greatly feared had at last come upon me. In the Trinity Term of 1929 I gave in, and admitted that God was God, and knelt and prayed: perhaps, that night, the most dejected and reluctant convert in all England."

His conversion to theism was only a rest stop. In 1931 Lewis had his famous conversation with Tolkien and Lewis' friend, Hugo Dyson. During a long walk around the grounds of Oxford, Lewis told Tolkien that although myths are powerful, they are ultimately "lies and therefore worthless, even though breathed through silver."

"No," said Tolkien. *"They are not lies."* At this moment Lewis remembered "a rush of wind which came so suddenly on the still, warm evening and sent so many leaves pattering down that we thought it was raining. We held our breath."

Tolkien continued by saying that even though myths contained error, there were also shards of truth. He believed in mankind's urge to "make myths," and the imaginative faculties to do so came from God. The storyteller, or "sub-creator", is "actually fulfilling God's purpose, and reflecting a splintered fragment of the true light. Pagan myths are therefore never just lies, Tolkien concluded: "There is always something of the truth in them."[7]

After Lewis conceded myths could have truth in them, Tolkien told Lewis that Christianity was a true myth, a myth that really happened. Tolkien shared with Lewis his belief

"that pagan myths were, in fact, God expressing himself through the minds of poets, using the images of their 'mythologies' to reveal fragments of His eternal truth...Tolkien maintained that Christianity was exactly the same except for the enormous difference that the poet who invented it was God Himself, and the images He used were real men and actual history...The old myth had become a fact while still retaining the character of a myth."[8]

No one had ever talked to Jack Lewis like this before. Shortly afterward he wrote a friend, "I have just passed on from believing in God to definitely believing in Christ - in Christianity. I will try to explain this another time. My long night talk with Dyson and Tolkien had a good deal to do with it."[9]

Middle Earth

Lewis' conversion to Christianity was the high water mark in the relationship between he and J.R.R. Tolkien. Tolkien had hoped Lewis would convert to Catholicism and was disappointed when Lewis joined the Anglican Church instead.

Nevertheless, Tolkien would write:

"Friendship with Lewis compensates for much, and besides giving constant pleasure and comfort has done me much good from the contact with a man at once honest, brave, intellectual - a scholar, a poet, and a philosopher - and a lover, at least after a long pilgrimage, of Our Lord."[10]

Another benefit Tolkien received was Lewis' fervent encouragement of Tolkien's writing. Both men had joined a group called the Inklings: literary men like Lewis' brother Warnie, Charles Williams, and Hugo Dyson. Tolkien said the name Inklings was a pun, "describing people with vague or half-formed ideas who also work in ink." Occasionally the gentlemen met at a local pub called The Eagle and Child, which they renamed "Bird and Baby." There they drank and argued about literature.

It was to the Inklings that Tolkien hesitantly began to read a work of imaginative Christian mythology he wrote called *The Silmarillion*. Lewis was captivated and became Tolkien's biggest fan. His heartfelt encouragement and constructive criticism caused Tolkien to believe there may be a larger audience for his fiction. In 1937 *The Hobbit* was published. The first edition sold out in three months.

Tolkien tried to interest his publisher in *The Silmarillion*. Write more about hobbits, they replied. With C.S. Lewis' constant encouragement, Tolkien began melding hobbits and the landscape of Middle Earth with the epic tapestry of *The Silmarillion.* The result was *Lord of the Rings.*

Tolkien wrote late at night in his small study with its erratic stove, scrawling with a dip-pen on the backs of old examination papers. He would read the finished chapters at Inklings meetings. Lewis was the most enthusiastic and the most critical. It annoyed Lewis that Tolkien seemed heedless to his criticisms. "No one ever influenced Tolkien," he complained, "you might as well try to influence a Bandersnatch."[11]

In fact, Tolkien *was* affected by Lewis' often harsh critiques - they injured him, and he responded by ignoring Lewis. Tolkien was a perfectionist, and he subjected his writing to as stiff an examination as he did his conscience before going to Confession. His writer's block was not aided by the onset of the Second World War, the bombing of England by Nazi Germany, and the enlisting of two of Tolkien's sons in the war.

C.S. Lewis' biographer declared:

"The greatest single goad to Tolkien's pen was Lewis. Month after month Lewis nagged Tolkien for more...

It could be said with almost complete certainty that we should never have had *The Lord of the Rings* had not C.S.L. been so anxious to read to the end..."[12]

"I needed some pressure," Tolkien admitted. He finished the book, originally titled The *War Of The Ring*, several years after the end of the second World War. Then came another massive revision, as he tried to end - or say goodbye - to the story. Finally, it was over.

The desk in his study was too cluttered, so Tolkien balanced his typewriter on his attic bed and typed out a copy of the complete epic - with two fingers, as he had never learned to type with ten. *The Lord of the Rings* was finished in 1949. Of it Tolkien said, simply, "It is written in my life-blood, be it thick or thin; and I can no other."[13]

Narnia

Lewis did more than just encourage Tolkien to persevere with *The Lord of the Rings.* He became a Christian radio apologist and an author during the Second World War. Recalling the combat required to move Lewis out of his atheistic foxhole must have given Tolkien and Lewis an appreciation of the irony in Lewis' sudden popularity as a Christian apologist.

During the war Lewis wrote perhaps his best book, *The Screwtape Letters*, which he dedicated to Tolkien. Next was a science fiction trilogy Lewis wrote wherein the main character, Ransom, was modeled after Tolkien, even having the same profession, philology.[14] This may have been in response to Tolkien modeling Treebeard's manner of speaking ("Hoom, Hom") after Lewis.

After the war, Lewis' fame as a Christian radio personality and author grew, at least among English speaking

Protestants. On the air and in print he reduced Christianity to the lowest common denominator in order to avoid squabbles between denominations. Lewis also ignored doctrinal differences between Catholicism and Protestantism. This led Tolkien to dub Lewis "Everyman's theologian." It was not a compliment.

In 1949 Lewis read to Tolkien and the other Inklings a book he called *The Lion, The Witch, And The Wardrobe*. Tolkien's reaction was immediate. He disliked the story intensely. Lewis' biographer recorded Tolkien's reaction:

> "I hear you've been reading Jack's children's story. It really won't do, you know!...I mean to say, *"Nymphs and Their Ways, The Love Life of A Faun."* Doesn't he know what he's talking about?"[15]

The seven slim books comprising C.S. Lewis' *The Chronicles of Narnia* would be published in a mere seven years. Tolkien had taken over a dozen years to write *The Lord of the Rings,* and now it languished at one publisher after another.[16] He was almost sixty and feared his labor of love would never see the light of day. It may have galled him when Lewis not only borrowed some of Tolkien's ideas but dashed off (what Tolkien considered) a sloppy, truncated imitation of *Lord Of The Rings that* sold very well.

As it turned out, both imaginary worlds become beloved around the world. Lewis helped Tolkien finish *The Lord of the Rings,* which in turn inspired Lewis' *Chronicles of Narnia*. While Lewis was always of fan of Middle Earth, Tolkien never had time for Narnia – even after sales of *Lord of the Rings* surpassed everyone's wildest expectations.

Afterward

The Inklings informally disbanded around 1949. Tolkien and Lewis were growing apart. The wedge was religious and literary. Tolkien was a traditional Roman Catholic who felt Lewis had not come all the way to the truth. Their literature and literary tastes had diverged from each other. Their lives seemed to be going in different directions.

A cause and effect of the separation was the stringent criticism they subjected each other's work to. After a particularly severe critique of Lewis'efforts, Tolkien wrote a letter of apology. Likening himself to "a savage creature, a sore-headed bear, a painful friend," Tolkien praised Lewis for his goodness. But they could not recapture the magic of their relationship.

In 1954 Lewis left Oxford to accept a position as chair of Mediaeval and Renaissance Literature at Cambridge University. In August of 1954 *The Fellowship of the Ring* was published. On April 23 1956 C.S. Lewis married Joy Davidman Gresham, an American writer and convert to Christianity. He did not tell Tolkien or invite him, probably because Lewis knew Tolkien would disapprove of Lewis marrying a divorced woman. Tolkien only found out about the marriage much later, from a third party.

Joy Davidman died in 1960 of bone cancer. Lewis grieved profoundly, to the point of questioning his religious convictions. He did not share his turmoil with Tolkien. On July 15 1963 C.S. Lewis had a heart attack and fell into a coma. He survived but was never the same. He died later that year on November 22. His death was overshadowed by the assassination of President John Kennedy on the same day.

Upon hearing of Lewis' death, Tolkien told his daughter he felt "like an old tree that is losing all its leaves one by one," and that Lewis' death "feels like an axe blow near the roots."[17] He soldiered on until 1973. While visiting friends in the seaside town of Bournemouth, Tolkien was hospitalized for a bleeding ulcer. An infection developed in his chest. He died with his children at his bedside on September 2, 1973, at the age of eighty-one. His son Michael, a Roman Catholic priest, performed a requiem mass for his father.

So ended the lives of two great storytellers. They have left us remarkable tales that continue to be told and retold. For many golden years John Ronald Reuel Tolkien and Clive Staples Lewis brought out the best in each other, gave each other remarkable companionship, exchanged profound ideas about life death, God, and the universe, and gave us an example of creative friendship that is inspiring indeed. We are all much the better for it.

Sources

[1] Humphrey Carpenter, *The Inklings, C.S. Lewis, J.R.R. Tolkien, Charles Williams And Their Friends*, Boston, Houghton Mifflin Company, 1979, p. 27.

[2] In 1925 Lewis had been granted a Fellowship at Magdalen College as a Tutor in English Language and Literature.

[3] Ibid., p. 13.

[4] Ibid, pp. 22-23.

[5] Carpenter, *J.R.R. Tolkien*, op. cit., p. 145.

[6] Carpenter, *The Inklings*, op. cit., p. 7.

[7] Carpenter, *The Inklings*, op. cit., pp. 43-44. The term "sub-creator" was Tolkiens. He used it to show the subordination of creature to Creator.

[8] Joseph Pearce, *Tolkien, Man And Myth, A Literary Life*, San Francisco, Ignatius Press, 1998, pp. 57-60.

[9] Carpenter, *The Inklings*, op. cit., p. 45.

[10] Pearce, op. cit., p. 60.

[11] Carpenter, *Tolkien,* op. cit., p. 201.

[12] See A.N. Wilson, *C.S. Lewis, A Biography*, New York, W.W. Norton & Company, (pp. 196-197).

[13] Carpenter, *Tolkien*, op. cit., pp. 203-4 for the quote and the anecdote about Tolkien's typing.

[14] Tolkien's daughter Priscilla also thought Ransom was modeled on Tolkien. "As a philologist," Tolkien said, "I may have some part in him and recognize some of my opinions and ideas Lewisified in him (Ransom). (Carpenter, *The Inklings*, op. cit., p. 182.)"

[15] Griffin, op. cit., pp. 296-297.

[16] One of the problems with the initial publication of LOTR was the sheer size of the manuscript, some 600,000 pages, which Tolkien insisted should be published as one book. Other problems included a post-war paper shortage that drove up costs and Tolkien's alternating bouts of perfectionism and procrastination during the publication process.

[17] Carpenter, *Letters*, op. cit., p. 341.

RELIGION AND SPIRITUALITY

The Triumphs And Trials Of Mahatma Gandhi

THE UNITED NATIONS General Assembly has declared October 2 the International Day of Non-Violence. This date is the birthday of Mohandas Karamchand Gandhi, better known as Mahatma ("great soul") Gandhi. His non-violent political activism has been emulated by Martin Luther King, Nelson Mandela, and the Dalai Lama. So what did Gandhi do to have a special day declared in his honor?

Born in 1869, Gandhi's love of truth was evident at an early age. His childhood hero was King Harishchandra, an Indian figure renowned for his piety and honesty. In his autobiography Gandhi said the story of Harishchandra "haunted me and I must have acted Harishchandra to myself times without number."

At age thirteen (1892) Gandhi married a fourteen-year-old Indian girl named Kasturba Makhanji. The marriage was arranged by parents and community members. Over the years the couple had four sons. Their marriage was often interrupted by Gandhi's travels. The first trip occurred when in 1898 Gandhi attended law school in London, England.

Law school was the idea of Gandhi's parents. Their son was an average student who struggled to pass his final exams at Samaldas College in India. When he left home Gandhi promised his mother he would be a vegetarian in England. This vow was the start of a lifelong passion for Gandhi.

Dissatisfied with vegetarian fare in London, Gandhi joined the London Vegetarian Society. His motive may have been an attempt to find better food to eat. Promises have a way of opening up whole new worlds, and this was true for Gandhi.

It was through the intellectuals of the London Vegetarian Society that Gandhi was introduced to the ideas of Leo Tolstoy and Henry David Thoreau. Even more importantly, Gandhi began to seriously read the epic poem, *Bhagavad Gita*, the most sacred and important text for Hindu Indians.

After studying in London for three years, Gandhi passed the bar exam on June 10, 1891, and returned to India to start his legal practice. Upon arriving home Gandhi learned his mother died while he was in England. His family kept the news from him, perhaps in an attempt to make Gandhi finish his studies without distraction.

For the next two years Gandhi struggled to learn Indian law. Another trial was overcoming an extreme shyness that made it difficult for Gandhi to be heard in the courtroom. His travels continued when he accepted a position as legal representative for the Muslim Indian Traders in Natal, a British ruled colony in South Africa.

Many Indians had migrated to British ruled South Africa. The impetus for the "Indian Diaspora" was economic. The rulers of South Africa needed cheap manual laborers, and many Indians were willing to start over again in South Africa. Although the British Empire had abolished slavery, the indentured servitude of many Indians in South Africa was simply slavery called a different name.

Gandhi's twenty-one year sojourn to South Africa did not begin well. He was thrown off a train after refusing to give up his first class seat to whites. He was beaten by a stagecoach driver for a similar offense. He was barred from hotels, and ordered to remove his turban, which he refused to do.

Gandhi responded to these episodes by becoming bolder in asserting his rights as a human being. In standing up for himself Gandhi was also standing up for something larger: his people.

It was in South Africa that Gandhi began to understand his fellow Indians, and as his mind penetrated the cultural, political, and religious complexities of his race, he envisioned a method to help his people fight for equality with the ruling classes.

Gandhi put his understanding to work in organizing groups and structures to empower South African Indians, creating roles for them in mainstream society. During the Boer War Gandhi organized the Indian Ambulance Corps to help wounded English soldiers. In so doing Gandhi earned the gratitude of the British Empire.

The philosophy behind Gandhi's political and social activities was something he called *satyagraha*: "truth force." The application of *satyagraha* was focused nonviolent resistance to a specific injustice. But there was more involved than passive resistance:

> "A *satyagrahi* (a person using *satyagraha*) would resist the injustice by refusing to follow an unjust law. In doing so, he would not be angry, would put up freely with physical assaults to his person and the confiscation of his property, and would not use foul language to smear his opponent.

> "A practitioner of *satyagraha* also would never take advantage of an opponent's problems. The goal was not for there to be a winner and loser of the battle, but rather, that all would eventually see and understand the "truth" and agree to rescind the unjust law." (see sources for citation)

Gandhi's ideals were put to the test when he organized nonviolent resistance to "The "Black Act," a 1907 law which required all Indians to be fingerprinted and have their registration paperwork with them wherever they went. Under Gandhi's direction, Indians refused to get fingerprinted and peacefully picketed government offices. It took seven long years, but Gandhi's application of *satyagraha* triumphed when "The Black Act" was repealed.

When Gandhi returned to India for good in 1915, he came as a hero with a worldwide reputation for principled activism. He was given the honorary title "Mahatma", or "great soul." Many Indians considered Gandhi a holy man and a saint. Such titles made Gandhi cringe; he saw himself as quite an ordinary man.

Gandhi joined the Indian National Congress during the First World War. By 1920 he was leader of the Congress. He began using the tactics he developed in South Africa. There were problems when large scale protests invariably turned violent. The violence came from Indians, not the British.

Another form of violence was based on the religious differences between Indian Hindus and Muslims. Upon being released from prison (for sedition) Gandhi did personal penance for the violence, going on a 21 day fast. He nearly died halfway through, but revived to finish what was later called "the Great Fast of 1924." It resulted in a temporary truce between India's Hindus and Muslims.

In 1930 Gandhi and the Indian National Congress declared the independence of India from British rule. The British refused to recognize Indian independence, but subsequent negotiations led to Congress having a role in the British rule in India. In 1942 Gandhi demanded immediate independence from British rule, and was immediately jailed, along with many members of the Congress.

Gandhi was released in 1944. His *satyagraha* policies

were effective against the British government, but proved no antidote to the Muslim-Hindu violence between his countrymen that reached such epidemic proportions that in 1947 Britain willingly left India.

The British exit strategy was a partition: northern territories of India would be home to India's Muslims, who renamed their land Pakistan. The rest of India belonged to the majority Hindus. Gandhi opposed the partition, but his was a lonely voice. By the end the British were not the enemy: Indians were at war with themselves.

Once more Gandhi fasted to stop the violence. He was so loved by Hindus and Muslims that both sides quickly called a truce for fear that Gandhi would not live through his latest fast. Gandhi lived for another six months. Then on January 30 1948 he died – but not from fasting. A Hindu nationalist who despised Mahatma's non-violent principles fired three bullets into Gandhi's chest, killing him immediately.

All of India went into mourning for their beloved "Bapu" ("father"). Gandhi's great success was to help India achieve independence. Although his memory is revered today, modern India pays no heed to the ideals of *satyagraha.* This would not have surprised Gandhi. He knew his ideals were hard for most people to follow. Yet he insisted to the last that his philosophy and methods were merely part of the natural law of the universe:

"There is no such thing as "Gandhism", and I do not want to leave any sect after me. I do not claim to have originated any new principle or doctrine. I have simply tried in my own way to apply the eternal truths to our daily life and problems...

"The opinions I formed and the conclusions I have arrived at are not final. I may change them tomorrow.

I have nothing new to teach the world. Truth and non-violence are as old as the hills. (see Sources)"

While there may not be "Gandhism," there are a wealth of expressions attributed to Gandhi, such as:

"An eye for an eye ends up making the whole world blind."

"First they ignore you, then they laugh at you, then they fight you, then you win."

"Anger and intolerance are the enemies of correct understanding."

If patience is worth anything, it must endure until the end of time. A living faith will last in the midst of the blackest storm."

"Be the change you wish to see in the world."

"Nobody can hurt you without your permission."

Sources

https://www.britannica.com/biography/Mahatma-Gandhi

https://www.biography.com/activist/mahatma-gandhi

https://www.thoughtco.com/interesting-gandhi-facts-1458248

https://www.azquotes.com/author/5308-Mahatma_Gandhi

https://www.history.com/topics/india/mahatma-gandhi

The Rags To Riches True Life Story of Manny Pacquiao

OUR MAN OF the hour hails from a metropolis on the south-ernmost end of the Philippine archipelago called General Santos City. GenSan, as it is more commonly known, is a living, breathing example of the extremes in the Philippine world. Steel and glass buildings shine, shimmer, and seem to sweat in the broasting heat. In the shadow of these monuments to progress and commerce lies the other side of GenSan: an overpopulated third world tin shanty slum whose inhabitants labor under crushing poverty.

This is where Emmanuel Dapidran Pacquiao was born on December 17 1978. As an addendum to his baptism he also received the inevitable shortening of his name to "Manny." He is the fourth of six children born to Rosalio Pacquiao and Dionesia Dapidran-Pacquiao. Rosalio Pacquiao worked for a time in a different city from his family (not uncommon in the Philippines) to better support them. Rosalio liked the other city so much he settled there with another woman, and in the process of starting a second family forgot all about his first one.

The legend is that Manny never knew his father until

the man appeared one day, killed Manny's dog, ate it, then disappeared again. The truth is as murky as the legend, but according to Manny his dad was around until Manny was ten. Manny also says yes, dad ate his dog - but he didn't kill it. So there.

Small surprise young Pacquiao sped away from GenSan (well, chugged away on a boat anyway) to the great northern city of Manila. He thought it would help his family if his mother didn't have to provide for him. Dionesia had separated from Rosalio (divorce is illegal in the Philippines) and struggled to feed the hungry mouths. So Manny was probably sincere about helping his family, but he may have also thought he would have better luck elsewhere, both for himself and his family.

Family is sacred to Filipinos. They look after their own - one way or another. The great Philippine diaspora includes many Filipinos who separate from their family to work abroad in order to benefit their families with more favorable overseas wages than the cruel Philippine economy will yield.

At any rate, the fourteen year old boy's diaspora from GenSan to Manila was supported by a tremendous metabolism that allowed him to work countless jobs: construction, selling food, and running various errands until he was tired enough to sleep - usually under a bridge, with newspapers for blankets. Oh, and Manny learned to box.

It is a no brainer to observe that a boy so abandoned and mistreated by his father would want to punch other men. Punch them Manny did, in illegal back alley affairs for a dollar or two a fight. In the gym Pacquiao failed to impress. Trainers thought him a marginal local talent. Nevertheless, he made the Philippine national amateur boxing team, an organization that not only trained Pacquiao, but provided room and board too.

Manny blossomed under regular training. His amateur record was 60-4. At sixteen he turned pro: all four feet eleven inches and ninety eight pounds of him. The problem was he wasn't big enough to fight anyone. Pacquiao weighted his trunks to fight in the lightest boxing division (junior flyweight). But no one cared because Pacquiao didn't matter.

People started to care when he kept winning fights he was supposed to lose. How was Pacquiao able to beat bigger, more experienced fighters? Manny hit hard but he was not a knockout artist. His talent was in the incredible amount of punches he threw, and his uncanny knack for getting streams of his punches through his opponent's defense - round after round. Manny came out swinging and didn't stop.

At age nineteen Pacquiao migrated to Thailand to fight for a world title. He was an unknown when he squared off with world flyweight champion Chatchai Sasakui. The champ outclassed Pacquiao round after round until near the end of the fight when Pacquiao smacked Sasakui with a home run left hook that left the champ laying. Emmanuel Dapidran Pacquiao was a world champion.

But Pacquiao physically outgrew the flyweight division. When he couldn't make weight anymore and lost the title, Pacquiao moved up to the super bantamweight division. When boxers move up in weight they notice their opponents are bigger, hit harder, and take a punch better. It is tough to move up weights and fight bigger fighters, much less beat them all and win the division's championship belt. A few boxers, like Thomas Hearns, did it. Pacquiao is even more successful than Hearns. Moving up in weight and winning championships became Pacquiao's' trademark, and will probably be his legacy as well.

Another legacy began - outside the ring. Pacquiao met

a girl at a mall in GenSan. She was selling beauty products. He bought something he didn't need from her. He came back the next day and did the same thing. And the next day. Finally Manny asked her out. She said yes. Her uncle, a part time trainer of Pacquiao, chaperoned the couple. It was love at first sight. Pacquiao broke off his engagement to another girl to pursue his new love.

Her name was Jinkee Capena Jamora. Like Pacquiao she was a GenSan native. Jinkee dropped out of school to help her family out financially as a beauty consultant at a mall. When she married Pacquiao after a seven month courtship, she had no idea how much (and how soon) she really would be able to help her family out.

Jinkee became Jinkee Pacquiao in a civil ceremony in May 2000 - a ceremony shunned by Manny's mother, who waited to attend another ceremony done in the Catholic Church. Jinky remembers Manny as "just a simple guy back then." They began having children and raising a family. Then success caught up to the Pacquiao family.

Fame and glory increased with each Pacquiao victory. Fame pounded the Pacquiao family as relentlessly as Manny pounded his opponents in the ring. He became known as "Pac-Man" for his wrecking ball style: punches in bunches, crazy combinations, and precision shots from all angles that somehow got through to target. Manny out punched everyone he fought, and his crowd pleasing style made him a favorite around the world, including America.

It was a fight in San Antonio Texas that made Pacquiao world famous. He became only the second person to knock out Marco Antonio Barrera, which he did in spectacular fashion. It was a career defining fight. Jinkee remembers, "That time I feel that, 'Oh, Manny's really famous,' " she said. "This is not only the Philippines. This is the whole world. This is very different. So is our lifestyle. And the people surrounding us also."

Along with the fame and glory Manny had more money than he knew what to do with. So he started giving his money away to people: to anyone with a hard luck story; to the dubious thug life entourage that suddenly surrounded him; but most of all by gambling.

Pacquiao was a remarkably bad gambler. Promoter Bob Arum described him as "a degenerate gambler" who played several types of games and "always lost." Growing up with a poverty mentality, one might think Pacquiao would have clutched his money and saved it. But he threw money away like he didn't want -or didn't know how - to be rich.

Boxing champions are absolute chick magnets, and Pacquiao was no exception. He found himself overflowing in female companionship. Jinkee was often alone at home to raise the children. That certainly kept her busy, because the Pacquiao's are a fruitful union, with five children over the years: Emmanuel (known as Jimuel), Michael Stephen, Mary Divine Grace, Queen Elizabeth, and Israel.

Manny was wildly successful as a boxer. He has won a stunning ten championships in eight different weight divisions: something that has never been done in the entire history of boxing. He has been recognized by boxing authorities as the best boxer pound for pound in the world, and as the boxer of the decade (2000-2010). And he is the 2nd highest paid athlete in the world as of 2015.

But Pacquiao's success was destroying his marriage. To be precise, his reaction to his success came perilously close to breaking the bond between he and Jinkee.

Jinkee was tired of the affairs and the gambling. Her husband scheduled a reconciliation ceremony for the two of them and she was a no show. It may have occurred to Emmanuel Pacquiao that he was screwing up his marriage and abandoning his children just like his own father had. In fact Manny was worse than Rosalio because he had many more affairs. The elder Pacquiao did have one affair, but at least he stuck around to take care of the woman.

By 2011 the Pacquiao's marriage was on the ropes. Manny couldn't choose between his prodigal lifestyle and the woman (and children) he loved. Of course the act of not choosing is a choice. But maybe it was too late to even choose. Jinkee was talking separation, which could have excluded Pacquiao from his own family. It was crisis time. What would he do?

What happened next can only be described by Manny Pacquiao himself.

"I heard the voice of God and I saw two angels," he said. "When I heard the voice of God I felt like I died. ... I was in the middle of the forest and I was kneeling and praying with my face on the ground and then I saw a light, a very white light and I heard the voice."

Pacquiao was a cradle Catholic but in his entire religious life he had never had an experience like this. The heavens literally opened on him . He saw his career, his success, his money, and his political career (senator in the Philippine Congress) as so much straw. On his knees he cried out to the vision in acute contrition: "'I am not worthy in your sight. Lord just guide me."

As the Pacquiao's tell it, after the vision Manny went back to Jinkee and his family a new man. His religious experience saved their marriage. In Pacquiao's opinion, it also saved his soul. He considers himself born again, "convicted by the Holy Spirit" to use his words. And Pacquiao has not been shy in talking about how his conversion, or preaching and evangelizing through the sizable social media he has developed. Manny has become a man of God, a preacher.

The new preacher ran afoul of Western sensibilities by making volatile statements about gays and lesbians.

Pacquiao quickly apologized but not everyone was willing to move along so quickly - including Nike, who in a big time money move dropped their sponsorship of Pacquiao.

Freddy Roach has been Pacquiao's trainer for years. He has seen Manny in all sorts of situations, and he describes Pacquiao's current life like this:

> "It's (religion) more vital to him now than ever before. He was born a Catholic, now he's a born-again Christian. His mother [Dionesia] hates it. She's always trying to force the Rosary on him. The only worry about it is that maybe it could hurt his political career, because 90% of the Philippines is Catholic and he's a born-again Christian."

Fat chance it will hurt his political career. Pacquiao could run the country if he wanted to - he is that beloved by his fellow Filipinos. He is their fairy tale: a poverty stricken child becoming a multimillionaire.

But he is mostly beloved for his boxing success, and here is the snag. For Roach also notes Pacquiao has not been as successful in the ring since being smacked around by God. Conventional wisdom is that Pacquiao has lost his killer instinct. He is no longer the Pac-Man, he is a Christian minister and politician. If so, Manny has an entirely new venue to shine in.

Before that new chapter starts, however, Pacquiao seems to be crafting his last rodeo by scheduling a farewell fight with American Tim Bradley on April 9. This will be the rubber match between the two. Bradley was a careful choice. Pacquiao is confident he can win, and perhaps close out one of the most remarkable careers in boxing history. But even if Manny is able to leave boxing, expect to see him again soon in a spotlight near you.

Postscript

Since I wrote this article many things have changed in the life of Manny Pacquiao.

Pacquiao beat Tim Bradley by unanimous decision in April 2016. In November 2016 he knocked down Jessie Vargas on his way to another unanimous victory and the WBO crown. The following year Pacquiao lost his title in controversial fashion to Australian Jeff Horn. Most people watching the fight thought Pacquiao won. He landed 90 more punches than Horn but still lost the decision. No one expected Pacquiao to hang up the gloves on this sour note.

In July 2018 Pacquiao came back strong by scoring a technical knock out against WBA welterweight champion Lucas Matthysse. Pacquiao knocked Matthysse down twice and finished him in the seventh round. The victory was the 39 year old Pacquiao's tenth championship.

On January 19, 2019, Pacquiao retained his title by decisively beating four-division champion Adrien Broner at the MGM Grand in Las Vegas. The outcome was never in doubt as Pacquiao dominated his younger opponent. Afterwards Pacquiao said: "I'm still here in this sport. At the age of 40, I can still give my best."

His best is still very good. On July 20 2019 Pacquiao fought the younger, stronger, undefeated champion Keith "One Time" Thurman, again at the MGM Grand in Las Vegas. To the surprise of many, Pacquiao dominated Thurman to win a deceptively close majority decision. Pacquiao knocked Thurman down, bloodied him, and hit him with a body shot that had Thurman running for cover. Pacquiao became the oldest man to ever win the (Super) welterweight championship. Some commentators noted that the 40 year old Pacquiao fought like he was thirty.

So what is next for the champion? He wants a rematch

with Floyd Mayweather, but at age 42 Mayweather is unlikely to agree to a fight in which he has nothing to win and everything to lose - except of course, another huge payday. Some of Manny's fans worry about him persisting in fighting: they feel that their hero has nothing left to prove, and only leaves himself open to more head shots that could permanently injure him.

As things stand now, Pacquiao is at another career plateau, and can pick his fights and get more paydays he uses to build houses for his homeless countrymen. Pacquiao was a Senator in the Philippine government. He ran for President in 2022 but placed third. He remains however, the most famous Filipino in the world.

Sources

http://www.theguardian.com/sport/2014/oct/04/manny-pacquiao-chris-algieri-floyd-mayweather

http://www.nytimes.com/2013/11/23/sports/manny-pacquiao-working-out-a-stormy-marriage-that-came-with-bells-and-a-ring.html?_r=2&pagewanted=all

http://www.christiantoday.com/article/boxing.great.manny.pacquiao.from.booze.gambling.and.girls.to.a.devotion.to.jesus.christ/53156.htm

Myths Of The Flood

THE MOVIE *NOAH* revived interest in the biblical account of the Great Flood thousands of years ago. Yet virtually every civilization has a flood story of its own. The Hebrew story is one of many accounts of a great flood. Some other accounts will follow. When I use the word "myth" to describe these stories, I mean they are stories shared by a group of people as part of their cultural identity. Myth in this context does not mean true or false, and it is absolutely not used in a judgmental sense to discount any civilizations account of what is universally described as a harrowing experience.

The Islamic Koran recounts a version of a great flood similar to the Hebrew version:

Allah sent Noah to warn the people to serve none but Allah, but most of them would not listen. They challenged Noah to make good his threats and mocked him when, under Allah's inspiration, he built a ship. Allah told Noah not to speak to Him on behalf of wrongdoers; they would be drowned. In time, water gushed from underground and fell from the sky. Noah loaded onto his ship pairs of all kinds, his household, and those few who believed... The ship sailed amid great waves. Allah commanded the earth to swallow the water and the sky to clear, and the ship came to rest on Al-Judi... Allah told Noah to go with blessings on him and on some nations that will arise from those with him. (Koran 11:25-48)

The theme of mankind's wrongdoing being punished by the gods also appears in the Greco Roman version of the flood where, weary of the sins of men, Jupiter and Neptune conspire to wash humanity away by flooding the earth. The creator of mankind, Prometheus, warns the human Deucalion of the plot. Deucalion and his wife Pyrrha sail a boat to the top of Mt. Parnassus, the only spot of the world above water. There they throw stones behind their backs. The stones become people and the earth is repopulated.

The Lakota Sioux of North America tell of a time where "people didn't know how to behave or how to act human, and the creating power was displeased." The god sang songs to bring forth rain and "the earth split open, and water flowed from the cracks and covered everything." The god floated on the water on his huge pipe bag, which contained animals and birds. The creating power spread mud over the water, thus replacing the water with land. The creating power wept for the earth, and his tears became streams, rivers, lakes, and oceans. He created a rainbow as a sign he would not flood the earth again, but also warned mankind to be good. [Erdoes and Ortiz, pp. 496-499]

China's story of the flood is fundamental to Chinese culture, literature, and poetry. As usual, humans were misbehaving. The Chinese god ordered Gong Gong, the god of water, to create a flood. Gong Gong's flood lasted 22 years. Survivors lived high in the mountains and fought a day to day existence for survival. The hero of the story, Gun, stole growing soil and began to dam up the flood. The gods executed Gun but his son, Yu, sprang from Gun's corpse and forced the gods to give him back the growing soil. This was used to counteract the flood so people could come back down from the mountains and begin farming again.

China, in fact, did experience a great flood during the reign of Emperor Yao (approximately 300 BC). Chinese history books quote Yao saying:

> "Like endless boiling water the flood is pouring forth destruction. Boundless and overwhelming, it over-tops hills and mountains. Rising and ever rising, it threatens the very heavens. How the people must be groaning and suffering."

China's flood myth is unique in that it has a specific date. A version with a more general timeline is the best known myth in Western culture - the story of Noah and the flood:

> *God, upset at mankind's wickedness, resolved to destroy it, but Noah was righteous and found favor with Him. God told Noah to build an ark, 450 x 75 x 45 feet, with three decks. Noah did so and took aboard his family (8 people in all) and pairs of all kinds of animals (7 of the clean ones). For 40 days and nights, flood waters came from the heavens and from the deeps, until the highest mountains were covered. The waters flooded the earth for 150 days; then God sent a wind and the waters receded, and the ark came to rest in Ararat. After 40 days, Noah sent out a raven, which kept flying until the waters had dried up. He next sent out a dove, which re-turned without finding a perch. A week later he set out the dove again, and it returned with an olive leaf. The next week, the dove didn't return. After a year*

and 10 days from the start of the flood, everyone and everything emerged from the ark. Noah sacrificed some clean animals and birds to God, and God, pleased with this, promised never again to destroy all living creatures with a flood, giving the rainbow as a sign of this covenant. (Genesis, Chapters 6-9).

Scripture scholars contend the biblical Great Flood occurred sometime within the last five centuries, perhaps somewhere between 2000 and 3000 BC. There is no timeline in the Hindu scriptures regarding the first human, Manu, negotiating with a fish. In return for protection by Manu from larger fish, the fish promises to protect Manu from an impending deluge. The fish is really the Lord Vishnu, who floods the world to vanquish moral depravity. The virtuous Manu is the sole survivor. He makes an offering to the Lord and from this offering a woman appears, making repopulation possible. A new generation of humans begins, under the moral code of the caste system.

The major flood myths blame mankind's wickedness for provoking God (or gods) to punish ill deeds with a massive flood. When humanity has suffered enough God is appeased, and everyone gets to start over. An exception to the wicked man/angry God theme is a Babylonian flood myth in which the deluge is the god's solution for human overpopulation. One of the gods (Enki) told a man (Atrahasis) to build a boat for his family and animals. After the flood ended the gods took further precautions against overpopulation by creating stillbirths and miscarriages, and by making some women barren.

Flood myths come to us from all over the world. The Philippine islands have at least six different flood stories. Australia has fifteen. Africa has dozens, as does North America. The Mayans, Egyptians, Celtics, Aztecs and Sumerians all have myths of a Great Flood. It is logical to theorize that all these flood myths are based on an actual event in human history.

For instance, a catastrophic flood would explain the extinction of dinosaurs. It would explain numerous discoveries of seashells in mountain ranges, and fossil records consistent with a catastrophic geological event in Earth's history. Many flood myths record water flooding not just from the sky but gushing up from the oceans. Flood geologists theorize that before the Flood there were interconnected subterranean caverns of water, tightly compressed beneath the earth's crust. If a split occurred in the crust it could possibly run around the entire earth, causing the compressed waters to pour up from below. Such an event would change the face of the earth, and perhaps explain how parts of the earth are land and parts are water.

Flood geology is a branch of creation science scorned by the professional scientific community as a pseudo-science. Anthropologists claim that all the accounts of a great flood are explained by the fact that most of the human population lives near water and unusually severe floods happen to everyone. Surely they are recorded by each civilization's historians, but each flood is a separate event, not a worldwide flood.

But how do we explain the large boat resting 4,600 meters above sea level on the snowline of Mount Ararat? The area, which is on the border between Turkey and Armenia, is covered in ice much of the year, and threats of avalanche are omnipresent. Nevertheless, it has been visited by more than three dozen explorers over the centuries, including Marco Polo in 1269.

In 1840 an earthquake created a canyon on the side of the mountain the boat was resting on and shifted its position. During World War II American pilots flying over Mount

Ararat described a large boat-like structure on the mountain. In 2007 Turkish explorers climbed the mountain and filmed the boat from the outside and the inside. Nearly all flood myths involve a boat, but only one flood myth specifies that when the waters receded the Ark came to rest on Mount Ararat.

Perhaps something we can all agree on is that every civilization has its trials and traumas, be it wars, droughts, or floods. Rather than debate which story is "right", let us share our experiences and be stronger and more united for it.

Sources

R.C. Armour, *North American Indian Fairy Tales, Folklore and Legends*, (1905).

Campbell, Joseph, *Myths of Light: Eastern Metaphors of the Eternal*. Novato, California: New World Library, 2003.

Dundes, Alan (ed.) *The Flood Myth*, University of California Press, Berkeley, 1988.

Richard Erdoes and Alfonso Ortiz, Editors, *American Indian Myths and Legends*, Pantheon Fairytale and Folklore Library.

Mayor, Adrienne (2011). *The First Fossil Hunters: Paleontology in Greek and Roman Times: with a new introduction by the author*. Princeton: Princeton University Press.

William Ryan and Walter Pitman, *Noah's Flood: The new scientific discoveries about the event that changed history*, Simon & Schuster, (1998).

Yang, Lihui, *et al.* (2005). *Handbook of Chinese Mythology*. New York: Oxford University

nationalgeographic.com/news/2009/02/090206-smaller-noah-flood_2.html

The Priest And The Titanic

THE SHIP WAS sinking. A deckhand urged the priest to get on a lifeboat. He refused. In the last minutes of his life he ministered to dozens of frightened people, hearing jumbled confessions and giving sweeping absolutions. Then the priest led them in the Rosary. Everyone, Catholic, Protestant, and Jew, recited with fervor: "Holy Mary Mother of God pray for us sinners, now and at the hour of our death..." Then waves swamped the boat deck and washed them all into darkness.

The priest was Father Thomas Byles. His body was never found but survivors remembered his courage and selflessness on that fatal night. How he came to be Catholic, then a Catholic priest, and finally a casualty at sea is an interesting story.

Conversion and Priesthood

He was born Roussel David Byles in England in 1870. His father, Dr. Alfred Holden Byles, was a well known Protestant minister. Three of Alfred's seven children converted to Catholicism.

Roussel studied mathematics and theology at Oxford. Dissatisfied with the theological shortcomings of his Congregationalist upbringing, he converted to the Church of

England. Yet he soon became dissatisfied with Anglicanism, writing his brother William:

> "I find myself unable to recognize the Anglican position. I do not, however, feel myself anymore satisfied with the Roman position. I have given up going to Anglican communion, and have postponed my ordination as a deacon."

Brother William had already converted to Catholicism, and the two had a lively religious correspondence. Roussel converted in 1894, an event of which The Tablet wrote:

> "He was to be received into Holy Mother Church and to make his first Communion on the feast day of Corpus Christi, surely an appropriate festival for one who had been led perhaps more by his devotion to the Eucharist than by anything else to the altar where alone the Eucharist has its dwelling."

In 1899 he went to Rome to study for the priesthood, and was ordained in 1902 as Father Thomas Byles. An intellectual of slight build and frail health, he was assigned to St. Helens, a small rural parish in Essex, England. Many of the parishioners lived miles away from church, and Father Byles would bicycle through the country in search of Catholic houses. The efforts took a toll on him, but Mass attendance at St. Helens increased.

Although Byles taught local boys how to box in a barn behind the Church, he was more of an intellectual athlete, a thinker and a writer. He had a nervous disposition, and could be argumentative. A nearby priest who knew Byles thought so, anyway, but also observed:

"All his work was good, in the judgment of all, whether conference papers, or the ensuing debates, or public controversy. A thorough grasp of facts, exact reasoning, and clear enunciation of conclusions characterized his writing. In a word he was just what one would expect a scholar of Balliol to be."

No one knew if Father Byles experienced internal rebellion at being placed in the rural outback. He appears to have been committed to St. Helens and his parishioners, expending all his energies for their spiritual welfare. In a letter to another brother, Byles wrote:

"I wish I could impart to you something of the bliss of knowing with certainty what God has revealed for our support and help. It is a happiness that grows more and more every day and which affords a truly marvelous and altogether supernatural support in all temptation, and against all evil. It is however beyond my power to impart this – the most I can do is to pray God to give to all I love this wonderfully great Gift which I have received..."

Father Byles' brother, William, studied with the Jesuits until he realized he did not have a religious vocation. He relocated to America and became president of a business. In 1912 William wrote his brother to ask him to celebrate a wedding Mass in New York for William and his fiancée. Father Byles agreed, and booked ship transport to New York through White Star Line, a major British shipping firm. When he received his ticket he saw he was booked for the maiden voyage of the sensational new ship, the *RMS Titanic.*

The "Ship of Dreams"

Transporting people across the ocean was a lucrative business. There were growing numbers of wealthy travelers, and even more immigrants wishing to come to America. There was fierce competition for passengers between shipping lines in England and Germany. The idea for the *Titanic* grew out of this competition.

Originally, White Star Line intended the *Titanic* (and sister ship, the Olympic) as a response to arch-rival Cunard's introduction of the *Lusitania*, the fastest, most elegant ocean liner in the world at that time. Bankrolled by American millionaire J.P. Morgan, White Star Line created plans for a ship whose size, luxury, and modern conveniences would be on a hitherto unimagined scale. In the shipyards of Belfast, Ireland, fifteen thousand men began building the *Titanic.*

Three years later the largest moving object ever constructed was near completion. An observer described the *Titanic* as a ship "so monstrous and unthinkable that it towered over the buildings and dwarfed the very mountains by the water...A rudder as big as a giant elm tree, propellers the size of windmills – everything was on a nightmare scale."

The ship was the length of three football fields, and weighed over 46,000 tons. Three anchors, each weighing 15 tons, were required to slow it. Each link in the anchor chain weighed 175 pounds. The rudder weighed over twenty thousand pounds. Twenty-nine boilers, each large enough to house a double-decker bus, were fed daily the 5,000 pounds of coal required to move the ship.

Dubbed "the monster of the sea," when fully completed the *Titanic* was as elegant as she was powerful. Architect Thomas Andrews spared no expense to ensure the comfort of the ship's wealthy customers. A Turkish bath, a squash court, gymnasium, and a special dining room for maids and valets were some of the features.

Expansive, winding staircases, ornate imported wood paneling, luxurious carpeting, glass-domed ceilings, a telephone system, world-class cuisine, and other detailed amenities made first-class accommodations on the Titanic equal to that of luxury hotels.

The *Titanic's* captain, E.J. Smith, declared: "I cannot imagine any condition which would cause the ship to founder...Modern ship-building has gone beyond that." Noting the ship's watertight design, an engineering magazine declared that the *Titanic* "embodied all that judgment and knowledge could devise to make her immune from all disaster." A seaman spoke for many when he said, "God Himself could not sink this ship."

Some called the *Titanic* "a monstrous floating Babylon." More commonly she was called "the ship of dreams": for the undreamed of luxury afforded its first class passengers, and for the dreams of a new life offered to its third class passengers – mostly immigrants seeking their fortunes in America. The maiden voyage of the *Titanic* included a cross-section of humanity: millionaires like John Jacob Astor, celebrities, politicians, and hungry immigrants from Ireland, France, Germany, Eastern Europe, Scandinavia, Croatia, and Syria. Everyone knew they were part of an historic event.

Father Byles boarded the *Titanic* in Southampton. From his second class lodgings he wrote a letter to his parish housekeeper, Miss Field. After complaining about losing his umbrella, Fr. Byles described the ship:

> "There are eight decks above the water line. When you look down at the water from the top deck it is like looking from the roof of a very high building. The English Channel was decidedly rough to look at , but we felt it not more than when we were in Southampton

water. I do not much like the throbbing of the screws (the ship's engine), but that is the only motion we feel ...I will write as soon as I get to New York."

Setting Sail

Father Byles' letter was dated April 10, 1912. The next day the Titanic set sail from Southampton and was immediately threatened with mishap. Upon leaving her berth, the wake from the great ship broke the moorings holding another ship at dock. This ship, the New York, headed straight for the Titanic, and only fast work by the crew averted a collision.

The near accident was soon forgotten. The sun was shining and the ocean was calm. "I enjoyed myself," wrote Colonel Gracie, "as if I were in a summer palace on the seashore, surrounded with every comfort – there was nothing to indicate or suggest that we were on the stormy Atlantic Ocean." The sea was so calm Captain Smith opened the throttle. For the next two days the Titanic cruised at 24 knots over a glass-like ocean.

There was another reason for the increase in speed. Captain Smith was being badgered by Bruce Ismay, the managing director of White Star Line, to get the Titanic to New York faster than her sister ship, the Olympic. Crew and passengers recalled a conversation in which an animated Ismay repeatedly told Smith: "The machinery is bearing the test, the boilers are working well. We will make a better run tomorrow. We will beat the Olympic and get into New York on Tuesday!" Smith nodded without comment.

Father Byles strolled the boat deck in his cassock, reciting his Breviarium Romanum. Sunday, April 14, was Low Sunday, the Sunday after Easter. He said Mass for the second class passengers, and another Mass for the third class.

Speaking in English and French, he talked about being spiritually prepared. He likened their lifebelts to prayer and the sacraments, and warned them to be on guard against spiritual shipwreck. It was a likely enough sermon to preach on an ocean liner. Whether Father Byles' had a premonition of danger will never be known.

Throughout that day the Titanic had been receiving warnings from other ships about large ice fields. The month of April was notorious for icebergs, which broke off from Greenland and floated into shipping lanes in the north Atlantic. The Titanic changed its course slightly southward, but did not slow down. Sunday night was beautiful – a cloudless sky and remarkably calm sea.

As evening progressed the temperature fell to freezing and the air turned hazy. Experienced seamen knew these were signs icebergs were nearby. They were hard to see; the crew watched for white foam created when water washed against a berg. Visibility worsened, and the horizon blurred into the ocean. At 11:40 pm a lookout in the crow's nest rang the bridge: "Iceberg right ahead."

The Sinking

The Titanic turned the bow (front) of the ship away from the berg, but an underwater spar jutting out from the iceberg scraped the starboard (right) bow side of the ship under the waterline for about three hundred feet. Father Byles was on deck reading his Breviary, and saw the berg pass by. Like most passengers, he thought nothing of it. Passengers in the lower decks heard a grinding noise that quickly stopped.

Later everyone assumed the iceberg ripped a gaping hole in the Titanic. In fact the berg made a few very small holes in the steel plating, and only buckled other sections of plating. The water pressure was so intense, however, that sea water began shooting through the holes at 7 tons (2000 gallons) a minute.

The Titanic's watertight design made it possible for her to survive if four of the watertight compartments were flooded. The damage had flooded five. The Titanic's bow began to lower. Captain Smith estimated the Titanic would sink within two hours. He ordered the lifeboats uncovered and lifebelts distributed.

This bemused most of the passengers. They did not know the Titanic was sinking and had no intention of leaving the "ship of dreams" for a little wooden lifeboat in the cold dark sea. The band played on. Men smoked, drank, and played cards. Women refused orders to enter the lifeboats. No general warning had been given, and the crew did not announce the ship was sinking. When someone asked what was wrong, a crew member joked: "We have only been cutting a whale in two." Many passengers scoffed at the danger. "What do they need of lifeboats?" one woman asked. "This ship could smash a hundred icebergs and not feel it. Ridiculous!" Consequently, many of the lifeboats were launched only half full.

An hour after the collision the Titanic launched distress rockets, and a sense of unreality set in. Stewards were preparing dining tables for breakfast, while the band was wearing lifebelts and playing lively tunes. Ship engines had stopped but the ship was still fully lighted. "There was a sense of the whole thing being a dream," remembered a survivor. "That those who walked the decks or tied one another's lifebelts on were actors in a scene, that the dream would end soon and we would wake up."

Others began to take things more seriously, and willingly boarded lifeboats. The original plans called for sixty-four wooden lifeboats, but that was halved, then halved again to sixteen, partly to allow more room on deck for passengers, and partly from the assumption that lifeboats would not be needed. Even if the sixteen lifeboats had been filled to capacity, less than half of the 3,547 passengers could have used them.

When Father Byles realized the ship was sinking, he hurried down to the third class rooms to calm the people, bless them, and hear confessions. A survivor recalled:

"We saw before us, coming down the passageway, with his hand uplifted, Father Byles. We knew him because he had visited us several times on board and celebrated Mass for us that very morning. 'Be calm my good people,' he said, and then he went about the steerage giving absolutions and blessings.

"A few around us became very excited and the priest again raised his hand and instantly they were calm once more. The passengers were immediately impressed by the absolute self control of the priest. He began the recitation of the Rosary. The prayers of all, regardless of creed, were mingled, and all the responses, 'Holy Mary', were loud and strong. One sailor warned the priest of his danger and begged him to board a boat. Father Byles refused."

Another survivor, Bertha Moran, remembered, "Continuing the prayers, he led us to where the boats were being lowered. Helping the women and children in, he whispered to them words of comfort and encouragement."

After helping to load the lifeboats Father Byles was again ordered to get in. Again he refused. Helen Mary Mocklare said: "Father Byles could have been saved, but he would not leave while one was left, and the sailor's entreaties were not heeded. After I got in the boat, which was the last one to leave, and we were slowly going further away from the ship, I could hear distinctly the voice of the priest and the responses to his prayers."

Another man who refused to leave was Thomas Andrews,

the architect of the Titanic. He stood alone in the first class smoking room, ignoring requests to put on a lifebelt. His eyes were fixed on a painting entitled 'The Approach of the New World.' He was left alone with his thoughts. His labor of love lost, perhaps it was a relief for him to go down with the ship.

So did Captain Smith, who was last seen at the bridge around 2 a.m., watching the Titanic's bow disappear into the black ocean. The lifeboats were gone. The remaining passengers ran uphill to the stern, which rose high above the water as the bow sank further down. Father Thomas Byles continued to hear confessions, and then began the Rosary again. With a tremendous rending crack the Titanic split in half. The front half of the ship disappeared into blackness and the lights went out.

The stern settled down in the water, and floated until its compartments filled with water. Then the stern rose up from behind until it was almost perpendicular to the water, the rudder pointing at the stars. Most of the remaining passengers slid, fell, or jumped off. The stern remained straight up for a minute or two, as if in a silent salute from the vanquished to the victor. Then it began sinking straight down, like an elevator, picking up speed as it went down, down, down: plummeting more than two miles to the bottom of the North Atlantic off the coast of Newfoundland. It sits there today, as nature continues its slow victory by eating away the remains of the "Ship of Dreams."

Aftermath

After the *Titanic* disappeared all was quiet except for the screams, which one survivor chillingly referred to as "the chanting of locusts." Thus did the living distance themselves from the dead and dying. The forlorn cries died away after half an hour, as the luckless souls succumbed to hypothermia in the 28 degree water. There were so many bodies that the lifeboats had trouble getting through them to the rescue ship that arrived a few hours later.

The iceberg that hit the *Titanic* was seen later that morning. It had a long red streak of paint across it. It was not a large berg, at least the part above the water. For the next few days, as rescue operations continued, other passenger ships heading for America passed by bodies floating in the water. Preserved by the cold, they could be seen in horrible detail, including the evening gowns and tuxedos. Many passengers of the Titanic, like Father Thomas Byles, were never found. Some sank, others drifted hundreds of miles away.

In New York Father Byles' brother William went ahead with his wedding as scheduled. A substitute priest performed the ceremony Father Byles' had so looked forward to performing. After being married the bride and groom went home, changed into black, and came back to St. Paul's Church that afternoon for a requiem Mass for the soul of Father Thomas Byles.

Sources

The main source for the life of Father Thomas Byles is a website managed by Father Scott Archer at http://www.route24.net/~sarcher/Byles.htm.

Don Lynch, *Titanic, An Illustrated History*, New York, Hyperion Press, 1992.

Susan Wels, *Titanic, Legacy of the World's Greatest Ocean Liner,* Tehabi Books and Time-Life Books, 1997.

Geoffrey Marcus, *The Maiden Voyage*, New York, The Viking Press, Inc., 1969.

Judith B. Geller, *Titanic: Women and Children First*, New York, W.W. Norton & Company, Inc., 1998.

From Puncher
to Preacher:
The Remarkable
Transformation of
George Foreman

GEORGE FOREMAN IS known today as jolly George the entertainer: a genial pitchman with a ready smile; a promoter of products and ideas; an ordained minister with his own church; five wives (not simultaneously); and five sons all named George. It is a remarkable transformation from where he came from.

George was born and raised in the infamous Fifth Ward of Houston, Texas: nicknamed "the bloody Fifth" for all the violence. He grew up with his mother and stepfather and six other siblings, a large clan in a crowded house that did not have a bathroom. George was a big tough kid who liked picking fights more than going to school. He walked down the mean streets of the Fifth Ward, wordlessly punching strangers in the face and leaving them lying dazed on the ground.

After dropping out of school at age fifteen George hung

out with gangs until he drifted into the Job Corps. There he learned to box. Boxing got young George out of the bloody Fifth and into the summer Olympics in Mexico City in 1968, where he won the gold medal in the heavyweight boxing division.

After his victory in the final match George waved a small American flag in the ring, a sharp contrast to the black fists raised by African American sprinters on the award platform. Foreman turned professional and spent the next five years knocking people out. By 1973 big George matched his record of 37-0, (34 by knockout) against the undefeated (29-0) heavyweight champion, Joe Frazier, in a title fight in Kingston, Jamaica. In what became known as the "Sunshine Showdown," Foreman demolished the heavily favored Frazier, knocking him down six times in two rounds to become the new heavyweight champion.

Foreman defended his new title against Ken Norton in Caracas, Venezuela. In the "Caracas Caper," Foreman destroyed Norton in two rounds. Norton and Frazier were the only fighters to have beaten Muhammad Ali. On October 30, 1974, Foreman met Ali in Zaire Africa for the historic "Rumble in the Jungle."

Foreman came into the fight a prohibitive favorite. There was fear he might actually kill the older Ali, who had so much trouble beating Frazier and Norton. But conventional wisdom got turned on its head when Ali knocked Foreman out in the eighth round to regain the championship.

Foreman's glaring, surly persona did not intimidate the ring savvy Ali, who got an assist from his trainer Angelo Dundee. Years later Dundee confessed to illegally loosening the ring ropes so Ali could lay on the ropes out of reach of Foreman's heavy-handed attack. Even so, Ali later admitted that at least twice during the fight he blacked out from Foreman's punches – he was knocked out without falling down.

Foreman wanted to be champ again, but in 1977 he lost a decision to Jimmy Young in sweltering Puerto Rico. After losing the fight George also lost himself. The twenty-eight-year-old big bad George Foreman who disdained religion and used intimidation and rudeness to navigate through the world disappeared. What happened?

Witnesses remember Foreman's small dressing room feeling like an oven. George described the heat as "smothering." Overheated and agitated, the big man paced. Then he passed out, fell down, and began a remarkable emotional, mental, and spiritual transformation.

Those with him thought Foreman was suffering from heat prostration or even heat stroke. Although his eyes were closed, George was wide awake. Later he recalled his experience at length:

> "I was transported into a deep, dark void, like a bottomless pit...I lost my perception of direction, and didn't know which way was up and which was down. This was a place of total isolation, cut off from everything and everyone...a vacant space of extreme hopelessness, like being dropped in the Atlantic Ocean with nothing to grab on to, a thousand miles from shore.

> "I knew I was dead, and this wasn't heaven. I was terrified, knowing I had no way out. Sorrow beyond description engulfed my soul... I truly felt this was the end of my life, and I saw – too late – that I had missed what life was meant to be about. I got mad, I was furious that I had fallen for the devil's lies and deceptions. I screamed with every ounce of strength in me, "I don't care if this is death. I still believe there's a God!

"Instantly, what seemed to be like a gigantic hand reached down and snatched me out of the terrifying place. Immediately I was back inside my body in the dressing room. I couldn't believe it. I wasn't in darkness anymore. Even though I had lost all hope of escaping, God had mercifully let me out."

Foreman is describing a "near death experience," where dying people have what they later describe as a supernatural experience. Invariably the person experiencing the near-death experience has a profound shift in how they view themselves and the world. Frequently they are changed forever, almost always in positive ways.

Foreman's behavior upon leaving Puerto Rico followed form. He abruptly retired from boxing and became an ordained non-denominational minister. He founded a church in Houston called The Church of the Lord Jesus Christ. Then he opened a community gym for troubled boys he called The George Foreman Youth and Community Center.

So big bad George the puncher became born again George the community activist and philanthropist. Then, as George tells the story, he ran out of money when his accountant drained his funds. What to do? George declared:

"Those kids needed me, and I wouldn't desert them. I'd just have to find another way to raise funds. And then the thought struck me: I know how to get money. I'm going to be heavyweight champ of the world. Again."

Guess what? In 1994 at the age of forty-five George Foreman became the oldest boxing heavyweight champion ever when he knocked out champion Michael Moorer in the tenth round. Foreman wore the same red trunks he wore when he fought Ali in Zaire twenty years previously. Fortunately, the trunks were elastic enough to accommodate the thirty extra pounds big George carried the second time around.

Foreman retired from boxing for the last time in 1997 with a professional record of 76 wins (68 by knockout) and five losses. He had made more than enough money in the nine years of his second boxing career to keep the community center open and to replenish his finances.

In fact, Foreman's main income in the 1990's was not from boxing. He became a profitable pitchman for "the George Foreman Lean Mean Fat-Reducing Grilling Machine." George made millions off infomercials, but the big payoff came in 1999 when the Foreman Grill manufacturer, Salton Inc., paid Foreman $137.5 million in cash and stock for rights to his name and image.

Besides the grill, Foreman's promoting of Meineke Car Care Centers grew the business to over 1,000 franchises. There are innumerable other projects: a clothing line; several books; a reality show featuring Foreman's wife, Joan, and 10 children, including five boys named George; a line of environmentally safe cleaning products; an exclusive line of personal care products; a prescription shoe for diabetics to prevent amputations; a restaurant franchise called UFood Grille; a stint as color man for HBO Boxing; and resident preacher at his church in Houston, giving the good word to his parishioners four days a week.

In short, from growing up in a shack without a bathroom, George has done alright for himself. It is even tempting to call his near-death experience and subsequent life changes not merely remarkable, but miraculous. That is George's opinion anyway, in his autobiography entitled *God in My Corner*. He firmly believes God personally intervened in that hot little dressing room in Puerto Rico and changed the course of George Foreman's life forever.

Christian readers of his autobiography will be heartened by George's experience. Other readers may find it difficult to tell where George ends, and his promotional personality begins. Atheists will scoff and attribute Foreman's change to the power of positive thinking. Perhaps, but here's some advice for the naysayers: don't let George hear you. Word is he still packs a punch.

Source

George Foreman (with Ken Abraham), *God In My Corner, A Spiritual Memoir,* 2007, Thomas Nelson Inc., publisher.

Huston Smith:
Spirit Chaser

HUSTON SMITH HAS had as remarkable a religious life as any human being of the twentieth or twenty first centuries. He lived a productive and lucid intellectual life deep into his nineties. Even in his dying breath Smith never got over his love affair with religions.

That's right. 'Religions' in plural form. For Huston Smith declared an affinity for most of the world's major religions. He has been a committed Hindu, a devout Buddhist, and a reverent Muslim. That is quite a spiritual palette for a Methodist missionary's kid born in Soochow China in 1919. One of three sons, Huston and his family moved closer to Singapore to better evangelize the masses.

Smith remembered growing up speaking Chinese with his brothers. He assumed every Christian family was missionary. While many people have bittersweet memories of their religious upbringing, Smith's memories are positive:

"The faith I was born into formed me...in my case, my religious upbringing was positive. Of course, not everyone has this experience. I know many of my students are what I have come to think of as wounded Christians or wounded Jews.

"What came through to them was dogmatism and moralism, and it rubbed them the wrong way. What came through to me was very different: We're in good hands, and in gratitude for that fact it would be well if we bore one another's burdens (Interview with *Mother Jones* magazine, see Sources)."

At age seventeen Smith came to America to become a minister. He intended to return to China for more mission work after graduating. Instead he became intrigued by the subject of mysticism. In 1947 Smith began following Gerald Heard.

Heard was also the son of a minister (Anglo/Irish). He came to America to write and speak about science, politics, theology, and philosophy. Of particular interest to Heard was the evolution of consciousness; an interest Smith grew to share. Then in the 1960's everyone became interested in the topic.

Gerald Heard was a true spiritual pioneer in the Western world of rationalism, materialism, and scientism. He spoke often about the schizoid western Christianity of his day: liberal Christians who tolerated everything but dogma and doctrine, and conservative Christians whose devotion to dogma and doctrine bred religious exclusivity.

Flying above and below this duality, Heard was one of the first champions of comparative religion. This was a subject Huston Smith would mine for the rest of his life. When Smith landed a teaching post in St. Louis Missouri, Heard encouraged him to contact Swami Satprakashananda, founder of the St. Louis Vedanta Society. Smith recalled:

"I was perfectly content with Christianity until Vedanta -- the philosophical version of Hinduism -- came along. When I read the Upanishads, which are part of Vedanta, I found a profundity of worldview that made my Christianity seem like third grade...

"Later, I found out that the same truths were there in Christianity -- in Meister Eckhart, St. Augustine, and others. But nobody had told me, not even my professors in graduate school. So, for 10 years, though I still kept up my perfunctory attendance at my Methodist church -- a certain kind of grounding, I think, is useful - my spiritual center was in the Vedanta Society, whose discussion groups and lectures fed my soul."

Smith spent the next ten years as a Methodist Hindu. Then Buddhism came along. Smith described this as: "another tidal wave broke over me. In none of these moves did I have any sense that I was saying goodbye to anything. I was just moving into a new idiom for expressing the same basic truths." Smith devoted himself to the study of Zen Buddhism under the rigorous Rinzai Zen master Goto Zuigan for the next ten to fifteen years.

Smith tells humorous tales of becoming completely infuriated trying to solve Zen koans. He even yelled at his calm, smiling Zen master. Eventually he got the hang of Zen.

In 1958 Smith was appointed professor and chair of the philosophy department at MIT. That same year his first book was published: *The World's Religions: Our Great Wisdom Traditions.* It became his most enduring (and best selling) book. Smith was professor at MIT until 1973. During that time his immersion in Buddhism transitioned into the study of Islam. He also experimented with taking LSD, again with an assist from Gerald Heard.

Heard introduced Smith to writer and spiritual savant Aldous Huxley. Huxley introduced Smith to Harvard professor Timothy Leary, who in turn introduced Professor Huston Smith to psychedelic drugs.

At the time LSD was legal, and its use was respectable (until Leary got stupid about things). It was not viewed as a recreational drug, but as a possible portal into the mystic world of religious experience. Using LSD was strictly controlled and the recording of experiences was documented and assessed using the scientific method.

Smith took LSD along with *Alcoholics Anonymous'* founder Bill Wilson. Both thought LSD might help bypass the "tyranny of the ego" and open the human spirit to direct religious experience. Smith's conclusion is a famous one:

> "The heart of religion is not altered states but altered traits of character. For me, then, the test of a substance's religious worth or validity is not what kind of far-out experience it can produce, but is the life improved by its use? That's the test."

Smith was next appointed to Professor of Religion at Syracuse University. Although he retired in 1983, Smith never retired from the study of religion. Bill Moyers hosted a PBS multi-part special entitled *The Wisdom of Faith with Huston Smith.* In addition, Smith's film documentaries on Hinduism, Buddhism, and Sufism have won international awards.

Smith has written over a dozen books on various branches of religion. He has studied and conversed with virtually all contemporary religious and spiritual minds, for instance Alan Watts, D.T. Suzuki, Krishnamurti, the Dalai Lama, Joseph Campbell, Ram Dass, and many others. After his retirement Smith became deeply involved in the study of Native American spirituality, and added a chapter on this subject to his *World's Religions* book.

About the only branch of spirituality Smith is publicly skeptical of is New Age. Despite his deep explorations of other religious traditions, and his belief in their validity as spiritual paths that lead to God, Smith still identifies himself as a Christian. He claims his parents "instilled in me a Christianity that was able to withstand the dominating secular culture of modernity."

His more recent works are passionate defenses of Christianity and an insistence that a belief in God was crucial to the welfare of humanity: "If we take the world's enduring religions at their best, we discover the distilled wisdom of the human race." Smith is a universalist, that is, he believes everyone is saved, and that God made special paths suited for the temperament and gifts different races.

While he decries religious fundamentalism (be it Christian or Muslim), Smith also claims to be a religious traditionalist. He believes in God. He believes there are religious rules which must be followed. He even expresses a belief in hell, though this is rarely mentioned. And for a religious traditionalist, Smith looks askance at organized religion:

> "Institutions are not pretty. Show me a pretty government. Healing is wonderful, but the American Medical Association? Learning is wonderful, but universities? The same is true for religion... religion is institutionalized spirituality."

In the end, Huston Smith's religion is difficult to classify. Is it possible to simultaneously be a Christian, Hindu, Buddhist, and Muslim? Is it possible to be a religious traditionalist and believe everyone is saved?

What comes through clearly in all his books, DVDs, and

interviews, is that Huston Smith was sincere and passionate about God. Also clear is that Smith was *not* a spiritual gadfly. He did not flit from one religion to another like a dilettante. When he studied a religion that religion became a part of him, and he became a part of the religion he was studying. Small wonder the Christian Science Monitor called Smith "religion's rock star." The Dalai Lama has remarked that Smith knew the "real taste" of religion."

Huston Smith died peacefully at his home in Berkeley, California, on December 30, 2016. He was ninety seven years of age. He remained alert, oriented, and in possession of a remarkable sense of humor his entire life. It is a rare man who can speak from the inside out on the major religions of our civilization. Rather than try to classify him religiously, it may be more profitable to simply enjoying Smith's "tales of wonder," and "chapters from a charmed life."

Sources

http://www.motherjones.com/politics/1997/11/world-religion-according-huston-smith

https://tricycle.org/trikedaily/religious-scholar-huston-smith-died-97/

http://hustonsmith.net/

http://www.hustonsmith.com/

http://hustonsmithcenter.org/

Dana Sawyer, *Huston Smith: Wisdomkeeper: Living The World's Religions: The Authorized Biography of a 21st Century Spiritual Giant,* 2014. This is the source of the quotation in the final paragraph.

Glimpsing Heaven

NOT THAT LONG ago Judy Bachrach was afraid of death. Not just for herself. Judy's mom had Alzheimer's and was drifting behind the dusty veils of dream and departure. Determined to face her fears, Judy started volunteering at a hospice that exposed her directly to death. It also exposed her to stories of people who died but came back to life with stories to tell.

Bachrach's investigation into death experiences and the growing body of science on the subject is chronicled in her book, *Glimpsing Heaven: The Stories and Science of Life After Death* (published by National Geographic).

Bachrach has impressive credentials as a writer. She is a contributing editor at Vanity Fair and a professor of journalism at John Cabot University at Rome. But when it comes to death we are all puppies, no? Death is what we don't want to talk about, it is what happens to somebody else, anybody else but us. True, there are poets like Gregory Corso who declare:

> *Spirit*
> *is Life*
> *It flows thru*
> *the death of me*
> *endlessly*

like a river
unafraid
of becoming
the sea

Brave, even inspiring words. Yet where are fair words at the grand moment, the final stop for all sentient beings? Who issues fine verse during the death rattle, the last desperate intake of precious breath taken in full view of fast imposing blackness? Hands clutch what they can. Then everything ends. It is over.

Except for sometimes. Because sometimes during a routine everyday death, life continues on a remarkable new level. How? Well, in the words of those who have returned, "something happened." The 'something' was life happening during and after death.

When Dr. Raymond Moody introduced the notion of "near death experiences" in the 1970's, it seemed this phenomena, if it was even real, was confined to the very few. No longer. With advances in medical techniques for saving lives, we have launched full bore into the age of Lazarus.

People die and are resuscitated every day. It is commonplace. Less well known is that up to 20 percent return with a memory of what happened when they were dead. A 1982 Gallup poll revealed that some 8 million American adults had such recollections. It is likely this is an understatement, as many of "the returned" choose not to share their experiences for fear of being ridiculed or thought mentally unstable.

Some doctors assert that if the Titanic sank today and the passengers gradually turned to blocks of ice, that many of them could be saved after they died (like Jack unfreezing and calling for Rose).

Many of the returned recount remarkable adventures

during the time they were dead. As more data is collected, two strands are evident. First, every returner's story has something unique in it, unique to that particular person. This gives the stories a variety and originality that makes them hard to classify. The second strand, however, is that many details of the events recounted can be classified because they happen to so many people. A comprehensive list of questions has been developed over time to verify if a person really had a death experience, and just what sort of experience it was.

Dr. Bruce Greyson is a psychiatrist who has studied death experiences for decades. Over that time he painstakingly developed what is now called "The Greyson Index": a list of sixteen questions returners answer to classify their experience. If they answer 'yes' to seven of the questions they are said to have had a valid death experience. Many of the returners answer yes to ten or more of the questions. Either way, the results are intriguing.

Perhaps the most universal commonality in a death experience is bliss. Quoting research on this subject, Bachrach notes: "In death, untrammeled bliss is the order of the day. Of the 189 respondents who possessed memories of their travels, 74 percent reported "incredible peace or pleasantness. And 57 percent felt incredible joy. More than half reported...they had clearly left the body and existed outside it. (p. 78)"

Bachrach's research brought her face to face with person after person who had died, experienced something while dead, then came back to their body, and their body came to life again. Although initially skeptical, she eventually conceded:

"That makes these people one up on the rest of us. They have befriended death after experiencing it, acclimatized themselves to the future...They don't know everything about death, of course...but they know something, and that makes them quite special, distinctive, - some might say, odd. But anyway, people apart. (p. 74)"

Not everyone is willing to concede death experiences are what they seem to be. Those with certain religious convictions cannot always accept that atheists and the non-religious can have an angelic experience that perhaps should be reserved for the more devout. Atheists and those who do not believe in an afterlife also look askance at death experiences.

Others try to explain death experiences away using science. They say the death experiences are merely hallucinations, phantoms with no significance caused perhaps by a lack of oxygen. Lack of oxygen is a common occurrence amongst the nearly dead, particularly those in cardiac arrest. Being in a vulnerable state, it is argued, makes it unsurprising for Christians and other spiritual persons to imagine they are with angels, as this fits their belief system.

Still others theorize that the body compensates for the dire death situation by creating its opposite in order to soothe the traumatized victim, a form of sympathetic shock. Lurking behind these arguments is the unspoken: those who claim to have died and gotten a glimpse of heaven have...ahem... mental health issues. A special sort of criticism is reserved for doctors who give credence to death experiences. They are judged "unscientific" by their peers - the medical field's version of Long John Silver's Black Spot.

Doctors supporting the science of death experience point out that a lack of oxygen causes anxiety and confusion,

not glimpses of heaven. Furthermore, no one can hallucinate without a functioning brain - something those who
come back to life after cardiac arrest do not have. Yet the
returned have detailed, often remarkable memories and
experiences that are precise and lucid. These experiences
seem to have occurred somewhere outside the non-func-
tioning brain. Where? How? Those questions and answers
don't fit the Western medical model. Even so, a growing
number of doctors maintain the stories of the returned are
more than mere "hallucinations."

Death experiences are subject to the same critical review as any other medical novelty. The veracity of such reports is something for doctors and the medical community
to hammer out over the course of years and decades.

The challenge may be to keep the discussion medical
and not personal, that is, disparaging those claiming to
have had a death experience just because you do not like
the idea. Perhaps such a knee jerk reaction can be traced
back to a basic fact: no one likes talking about death -
even the returned can be reticent about recounting their
experiences.

After all, the stories are, well, crazy. Take the case of
a forty-something man found comatose in a park. Heart
massage and defibrillation did not work. When he finally
got to the hospital the man was blue and cold. No breathing, gag reflexes, or blood pressure. When intubated the
nurse took out the man's dentures and stuck them in a
drawer of the crash cart. One week after being put in a
medically induced coma the man came to life. The doctor
called it a miracle. The patient was rational and oriented.
And he wanted his dentures back. He instructed the nurse
where to find them. When the nurse followed his instruc-
tions - Voila! - the dentures were found.

Then there is the case of Bill Taylor, who died and went

to outer space. He experienced an ocean of loving energy. He believed he was in heaven, "a place of no fear." He felt curious about the way the world worked. Questions popped into his head, and were immediately answered. The entire universe seemed to him to be "the ultimate of simplicity." He remembered thinking, "So this is how it works! It's all so simple! It's a lot of energy." Along with the energy were feelings of intense love and acceptance. Where did Bill go? He said he went "home." In his words, "You know you're home. You just know you're home. (p. 113)"

But Bill had to go back to his life as a human being on this whirling rock *we* call home. In the hospital he kept thinking "You don't die when you die!" At last he was able to share the good news with family and friends. But they dismissed everything Bill said as "just hallucinations" brought on by the medications he was taking.

Several features of Bill's death experience are classic, recurring features. The intense sense of well being, a deep, sweeping comprehension of the universe and our role in it, and the feeling that you are finally "home." Another returner, Brother Dunston (a monk), echoed Bill Taylor's words: "It's home. And you know it's home."

Not surprisingly, coming back to mundane human existence is resisted by many returners, including noted psychoanalyst, Dr. Carl Jung, who had a death experience after suffering a heart attack in 1944. He found himself floating in space and encountering a temple. He had the conviction that entering the temple would answer any and all questions he ever had about anything. As he made to enter the temple Jung's doctor appeared and forbade him entrance. In his autobiography Jung's bitterness was still palpable: "I was not allowed to enter the temple, to join the people in whose company I belonged....life and the whole world struck me as a prison and it bothered me beyond measure...(to return to the world)" Jung would have to endure another seventeen years of human existence.

Pamela Reynolds died on the operating table. Her body was brain dead so theoretically she could not think, see, feel, or hallucinate. But Pam was not in her body anymore. "I popped out of my head," she explained later. Later she also explained details of the surgery to the surprised medical staff, including the song that was playing in the background (Hotel California by the Eagles). But when your heart stops, so does your brain. So medically speaking, there was no way Pam could have the knowledge about the operation.

Pam had knowledge of other things too. While dead she saw an incredible light. She also saw her dead grandmother. Pam asked her if the light was God. Grandmother answered, "Oh no, baby. God is not the light. The light is what happens when God breathes." Then another relative shoved Pam back, back, all the way back into her body. Back on earth, Pam had definite opinions on life after death she shared with people who were dying. Pam told them: "Don't fear death. Death is a beautiful thing. You're going to a beautiful place." To her family Pam declared: "Death is an illusion...Death is a really nasty, bad lie. You shouldn't fear death."

It all sounds like an irreverence by Beat poet Gregory Corso, who pictured death hiding under the kitchen sink, pleading with all who will lend an ear: "I'm not real. I'm just a rumor spread by Life." By the end of her book it sounds like Judy Bachrach, though not picturing a whimpering death under the kitchen sink, does not fear death any longer either. Speaking of the returned, she says:

"They know what most of us do not know - not yet, anyway. Death is not the end. That is what every last one of them says, and frankly, I believe them. We don't know - yet - how long these death voyages last. It could be for a few hours or it could be, as Dr. van Lommel strongly believes, that it lasts an eternity. But right now his conviction is just that: a belief.

"This we do know, however. Delightful or distressing, something extraordinary is going on after life. The very fact that this something exists, that it is an indelible memory in those who return from the dead, and subsequently a force that exerts a profound influence on the rest of their lives could tell us a lot. Our minds will not vanish. We will be, for at least a while, maybe forever, curiously empowered in ways we never were while alive. We will be enveloped at least for a time, by comprehension. This is our future (p. 230)."

Now that doesn't sound so bad, does it?

The Holy Shroud Of Turin: Burial Cloth of Jesus?

With a lot of hope, and also with a little trepidation, I am happy to announce that a special exhibition of the Holy Shroud will be held in the Cathedral of Turin..." Cesare Nosiglia, Archbishop of Turin, Papal Custodian of the Holy Shroud.

MILLIONS OF CHRISTIANS around the world believe the Shroud of Turin is the burial cloth that covered Jesus' body in the sepulcher before his resurrection Easter morning. Over the centuries there has been controversy over the Shroud's authenticity, and its long life has become a source of legend.

The shroud itself is fourteen feet long and three and one half feet wide. The threads are handspun. The fabric is handwoven in a distinctive herringbone twill. Since most crucifixion victims were criminals, it was remarkable that one would be adorned with such a valuable piece of linen. More often the corpse of a crucifixion victim was left to the tender mercies of wild animals and carrion birds.

Yet St. Matthew stresses that one crucifixion victim was wrapped *"in a clean linen cloth"*(Matthew 27:29). Then his body was placed in *"a new sepulcher, wherein no man had* yet been laid" (John 19:41). The burial shroud was next seen by St. John on Easter morning. The linen cloth was no longer clean. It held the blood stains and complete body image, front and back, of the crucified man. That was all it held, for the man was gone.

The shroud was taken and hidden by Christ's disciples, and secretly venerated. In 726 it was moved to Edessa for safety reasons. Edessa deputies handed the Shroud over to the besieging Constantinople army in 944, in return for the armies departure. In 1204 it was Constantinople's turn to be on the wrong side of an army. French crusaders sacked the city and left with, among many other things, the Holy Shroud. Then the Shroud disappeared for one hundred and fifty years.

In the 1300's the Shroud popped up in Lirey, France. In 1532 the chapel the Shroud resided in caught fire. The heat from the blaze melted the silver lining of the reliquary protecting the Shroud. Today one can see burn holes where molten silver dripped onto the fabric.

After that the Shroud was moved permanently to Italy. The dukes of Savoy housed the Shroud in the royal chapel of the Cathedral of Saint John the Baptist in their capital city of Turin. The Shroud has been there ever since, which accounts for it being referred to as the Shroud of Turin (it is equally well known as the Holy Shroud).

In 1898 the Shroud was displayed in a special exhibition. What could be seen by the naked eye was a faint, full scale outline of a man. An amateur photographer, Secondo Pia, used a new invention, the camera, to photograph the Shroud. When he developed the film he discovered that the Shroud image was actually a "negative" image of the crucified man. The positive image showed up on the photographic negative. This new image was full of remarkable detail not visible on the Shroud fabric. This inadvertent discovery changed everything.

The photographic negatives revealed the stark, violent beauty of a savagely beaten man whose disfigured face bore a calm dignity. It was as if the Holy Shroud had waited patiently until mankind had the knowledge to make cameras in order to begin revealing its mysteries.

In the ensuing century, no archaeological artifact has been studied more than the Holy Shroud. Critics point to a 1988 carbon dating of parts of the Shroud fabric as medieval to dismiss the Shroud as a forgery. Others argue: what sort of medieval forger would have the technology to create a photographic negative and positive image on a piece of linen, or the patience to wait centuries for his genius to be discovered?

Researchers have used cutting-edge technology to discover astounding facts about how the man on the Shroud was tortured and crucified. There are blood rivulets that flow in the proper direction, scourge marks that perfectly match the sort of scourges used by Roman soldiers during Christ's life, and puncture wounds in the forehead from a crown of thorns. Medical examiners were astonished to find that the location of the puncture wounds and clotted blood on the image corresponded exactly to cranial veins and arteries known in anatomy.

There was another detail that seemed forgery-proof. Artists have always depicted Christ as having nail holes in the palms of his hands. The figure on the Shroud has a nail hole in his wrist. Medical examiner Pierre Barbet performed experiments putting nail holes through the hands of cadavers. The hand always pulled away from the nail when pressure was applied. But when he put the nail hole through a fold in the wrist (known as the "space of Destot") the nail was supported by surrounding bone and ligaments and did not give way when traction was applied.

On the Shroud image the nail wound is right on the space of Destot. Doesn't this contradict the biblical prophecy: "They have pierced my hands and feet"? Not necessarily, because anatomically the wrist has always been considered part of the hand. Would a medieval forger have dared to contradict traditional artistic depictions of Christ with holes in his palms for the sake of anatomical correctness?

The gospels mention a Roman soldier thrusting his spear into Christ's side. This is the experienced death blow of a soldier: the spear blade would enter the chest cavity and pierce the heart. On the Shroud image there is an elliptical wound on the right chest two inches long and an inch wide: large enough for a doubting apostle to thrust his fingers through.

The way the details of the figure on the Shroud corresponded to history, anatomy, and biblical accounts were remarkable enough to create a new branch of science: Sindonology, the study of the Shroud. Another recent discovery was the ability of the faint image on the flat linen to yield a three-dimensional head.

The History Channel aired a two-hour documentary in 2010 on the recreation of a three dimensional CGI image of the face on the Shroud. The results were startling. The graphic artists involved remarked on how impossible it seemed that a flat piece of linen could yield such an image that conformed perfectly to the strictures of modern technology.

How many corpses can transmit a three-dimensional image of themselves onto a burial cloth? Perhaps a research project could be done on this, but it is likely that this phenomenon is peculiar to the Holy Shroud. The body image on the Shroud is perhaps its greatest mystery: a high resolution, anatomically perfect three-dimensional image that is not absorbed into the Shroud linen but rests lightly atop each minute linen fiber.

Tests have proven the body image is chemically pure, that is, not created by paint pigments, stains, dyes, blood, or protein deposits. Furthermore, the body image is "non-directional", which means there are no brush strokes or any other indication the image was somehow applied to the linen by human hands. Really now, what man-made conjuring could account for a body image on linen being inherently high resolution?

Microscopic examination of body image fibers reveals tiny granules at the top of each fiber. The granular density corresponds to the distance from the body of a particular part of the Shroud. Somehow the body transmitted these granules to the fabric, even though the granules were not absorbed by the fabric. Scientists agree there was some physical force emanating from the body that created the body image on the linen: a "flash of irradiation", of light and energy intense enough to almost scorch the linen while leaving a picture for the world to marvel at. Christians would explain this by saying that at the moment of Resurrection divine life filled the body in an explosive spiritual and phys-ical event. For them, the evidence on the Shroud is proof of Jesus' victory over death.

On Holy Saturday, 2013, the Archdiocese of Turin re-leased high definition images of the Shroud online and on television. When magnified (on a tablet, for example), the images revealed details invisible to the naked eye. This was a controversial move by the Archbishop of Turin be-cause of concern inside the Catholic Church that showing images of the Shroud on TV and the internet might cause the holy relic to be commercialized or trivialized. Today it seems this concern was unwarranted.

At this point one might wonder: what does the pope

think of all this? Well, Pope Francis recently issued a statement about the Holy Shroud urging veneration of the object but did not say whether he thought it was the actual burial linen Jesus was buried in. In so doing he is following recent papal precedent. The Vatican has been skittish about the Holy Shroud since the 1988 carbon dating controversy and all the negative press about the Shroud that came after that. Even though today there are peer-reviewed papers being published that openly question the validity of the 1988 carbon dating, the modern Vatican follows its own course. In previous centuries popes took the Shroud's authenticity for granted.

The Catholic Church, as owner of the Shroud of Turin, urges Christians to venerate the Shroud and what it represents. As a practical matter, however, it doesn't matter to Christians whether the Shroud is real or not, because Jesus is real and everything he did is real and that is the essence of Christianity, not an ancient piece of linen. For Christians, everything is still true with or without the Shroud. However, the Shroud is a physical testament to Christians that their faith is not misplaced.

We humans are fascinated by mysteries, so scientists will keep researching the Shroud; graphic artists will keep trying to reproduce it; and millions of people will come to Turin each year for a glimpse of the Shroud through its bulletproof casing. Surely some who look upon the image on the Shroud will wonder: is the Shroud of Turin the most remarkable forgery in the world? Or does the body it held belong to the most remarkable man in the world?

Sources

Pierre Barbet, *A Doctor at Calvary*, Dillen & Cie, 1950, Roman Catholic Books, Harrison Pennsylvania.

Werner Bulst, *The Shroud of Turin*, The Bruce Publishing Company, 1957.

Mark Fellows, *A Second Coming, The Holy Shroud In the 20th Century*, 1996, The Remnant Press.

John Heller, *Report on the Shroud of Turin,* Houghton Mifflin Company, 1983.

Kenneth Stevenson, *Verdict on the Shroud*, Servant Books, 1981.

Ian Wilson, *The Shroud of Turin*, Doubleday & Company, Inc. 1978.

Frederick T. Zugibe, *The Cross and the Shroud: A Medical Examiner Investigates the Crucifixion,* Exposition Press, Inc., 1982.

Fire at Cathedral of Notre Dame

IT WAS 6:18 pm on Monday of Holy Week: April 15, 2019. Mass was being celebrated inside the *Cathedral Notre Dame de Paris* when a warning light on the smoke alarm panel turned bright red with the word *"Feu"* - Fire.

One of the two security guards on duty inside the Cathedral was brand new and working a double shift because his replacement didn't show up. He radioed the other guard to investigate for fire. The second guard misunderstood and left the Cathedral to inspect the sacristy in an adjacent building. He messaged back there was no fire. The new security guard assumed it was a false alarm.

A call was made to the manager of the Cathedral's security department, who quickly realized the source of the alarm was not the sacristy, but the attic at the very top of the Cathedral. The guards clambered up the 300 narrow steps to the top of Notre Dame. Bent double to catch their breath, they saw to their horror that the marvelous, intricate lattice of huge wooden beams - many of them centuries old from forests that no longer exist - this incredible workmanship known as "the forest" that had covered and protected Notre Dame for eight centuries was being attacked by a fire growing larger by the moment. Someone finally called the fire department.

It was now 6:48 pm. The flames had a 30-minute head start on arriving fire fighters, who were destined to fight a losing battle from the start. Undaunted, they prepared to use the Seine River for their hoses, and to be tested to their limits.

Truly, if not for the bravery and remarkable courage of Paris' finest, the entire Cathedral would have collapsed, and most likely destroyed many of the most sacred relics imaginable - like a splinter from the True Cross, and the Crown of Thorns said to have been jammed onto the Savior's head during his Passion.

The firefighters resolved to battle the blaze at the very top of Notre Dame. Many wore fifty pounds of fire-fighting gear, along with breathing masks. There were no elevators to the top. The firefighters climbed the 300 steps. Exhausted, they faced the inferno and trained their hoses on it.

Far below the life and death struggle in the attic, a growing crowd watched in shock and horror at mountains of smoke spilling onto the spire, and the glow of a large fire eating its way through the wooden roof.

Paris has long been a secularized city. But what became evident at 7pm on April 15th was that Notre Dame de Paris (literally Our Lady of Paris) - the vast twelfth century monument to the Age of Faith - was still the heart of the city, and in some ways, the heart of the world as well.

The Cathedral of Notre Dame fits snugly on Ile de la Cite, a small island in the Seine River at the exact geometric center of Paris. Notre Dame existed at the birth of Paris, and over the centuries changed shape and size just as the city of Paris did. Like many Parisians of the day, Notre Dame was damaged and scarred by the Revolution in 1789. The Cathedral continued to weather all the storms that blew through the city, including two world wars. Today's fare is calmer: the Cathedral hosts more than 30,000 visitors every day from all around the world.

The world comes to see Our Lady of Paris in all her weathered, spectacular glory: to marvel at the vast stained-glass windows; to view centuries of artwork by the masters; to ponder the flying buttress system of arched exterior supports; and finally, to sit in a pew and feel peace. *Notre Dame de Paris* had always been there for its people, and for everyone. Until now. Now the crowd of people were there for the Cathedral.

At 7:50 pm Parisians and people across the world on social media, where the fire was being streamed live, watched in horror as the huge spire of Notre Dame collapsed and crashed through the roof down to the Cathedral floor. The sound was described by one firefighter as "a giant bulldozer dropping hundreds of stones into a dumpster." (https://strangesounds.org/2019/07/notre-dame-fire-collapse-save-paris.html).

The gigantic spire consisted of 750 tons of heavy oak and lead. Its crash through the burning roof caused a tremendous fireball to shoot through the attic. The firefighters were crouched behind a wall when the fireball zoomed by and scorched everyone. How graced they were not to have been incinerated on the spot. It was time to retreat.

Some firefighters wept as they descended. Outside there was a wail of grief, and cries of horror at the sight of the spire collapsing into the church, destroying everything in its path. It seemed the Cathedral was doomed. How could an 850-year-old building could withstand the agonizing torture it was being subjected to without totally collapsing?

The tears of Paris were shared around the world. Social media can be a sheer pestilence, but at times it can unite people of all different races, languages, and beliefs into the best humanity can offer. Such was the case with Our Lady of Paris during Holy Week of 2019. In a moment of bitter unity the Cathedral itself seemed to weep, but they were tears of black ash and flakes of fire. Both were sent skyward when the huge spire crashed through the heart of Cathedral Notre Dame de Paris. Slowly they descended, like snowflakes from hell to confirm everyone's darkest fears.

As night descended police drones from the air showed that the fire on top of the Cathedral was in the shape of a fiery cross, with a hole in the middle where the spire used to be.

Ariel Weil is the mayor of the portion of Paris that is home to the Cathedral. He spoke for many when he said, "There was a feeling that there was something bigger than life at stake. It was like an end of the world atmosphere."(Notre-Dame Fire Investigators Focus on Short-Circuit and Cigarettes, *New York Times,* July 14 2019).

The firefighters regrouped from their defeat in the attic. They saw the wind was blowing the flames north across the Cathedral, towards the wooden supports that held the eight huge bells in the north tower. If the fire caused the bells to fall, their weight and size would make them gigantic wrecking balls that would cause the northern tower, the adjacent southern tower, and probably the rest of the Cathedral to collapse.

The plan was to climb the southern tower and train their hoses on the nearby northern tower to prevent the bells from falling. But the northern tower was already on fire, and the firefighters were still on the ground. The hoses still drew water from the Seine, but the pressure was not strong enough to successfully battle the flames in the towers.

Not all the firefighters were willing to try the desperate plan. The small group of volunteers for the task entered the blazing Cathedral knowing they probably wouldn't have an escape route. As they began a second, slow ascent, Parisians in the crowd began singing devotional hymns.

It was a desperate plan: a real "Hail Mary." If the firefighters could reach the southern tower and find secure footing, they could use hoses hooked directly into the fire truck, giving them increased water pressure. Then they could try to contain the flames in the north tower to prevent it from collapsing and the nightmare event of eight multi-ton bells crushing the old Cathedral.

They reached the top of the southern tower and established a working platform. Some of the team trained their hoses on flames licking at their boots from below. Others kept the fire on the roof at bay. This allowed remaining team members to train the last two hoses on the fire engulfing the north tower.

The platform the firefighters were on was weakened from their own weight and the effects of the fire. Things can't get much more dangerous than what they were attempting. In fact, this act was not just dangerous. It was supremely reckless: behavior from the heart, informed by the head, and aided perhaps with courage supplied from above.

Yet somehow, someway, the firefighter's heroism and remarkable resolve in the face of death carried the day. The flames in the north tower were quenched. The bells stayed in place. Although many grim hours of firefighting lay ahead, at 9:45 pm the *Cathedral de Notre Dame* was saved from its gravest threat.

Beneath the firefighters on the south tower another courageous contingent formed a line on the floor of the Cathedral, now full of charred wooden beams and covered with thick gray and black ash. A group of firefighters, police, and citizens worked to remove the sacred relics stored on the main floor. They succeeded.

Although the firefighters saved the Cathedral from immediate collapse, it was several more hours until Prime Minister Marcon went on television in front of the Cathedral to announce victory, and to vow: "We will rebuild this Cathedral together." (Emily Bowden, *New York Post,* July 11 2019).

Three days after the final flames were put out, Paris' firefighters were formally and publicly honored for their outstanding public service. For weeks afterwards grateful Parisians - and world travelers - showered the Fire Department with gifts and heartfelt thanks.

As for Notre Dame itself, a very slow and painstaking repair job is beginning. People still come by to pay their respects to the grand old building. In the words of the *New York Times,* "that sense of the cathedral as a living wounded entity has only intensified since the fire." (Fate of Priceless Cultural Treasures Uncertain after Notre-Dame Fire, *New York Times,* July 15 2019.)

As a temporary measure Notre Dame parishioners celebrate Mass at the nearby church of St. Sulpice. No stranger to fire, St. Sulpice was a blaze one month before the inferno of Notre Dame.

Although the fire at St. Sulpice was not as devastating as Notre Dame, damage was still estimated at over one million dollars. The fire at St. Sulpice is downplayed by the Church and its rector. The reticence over discussing the fire at St. Sulpice may be because police have determined the blaze was caused by arson.

Arson and vandalism are commonplace among French churches. The International Business Times reported that 875 Catholic churches were vandalized in France in 2018. ((https://www.ibtimes.com/notre-dame-cathedral-fire-not-arson-875-french-churches-vandalized-2018-2785886)

During the week St. Sulpice was set on fire, eleven

other Catholic churches were also vandalized. One church had the Eucharist desecrated, and a cross scrawled on the wall with human excrement. According to Republican MP Valerie Boyer, "Every day at least two churches are profaned." (Emily Bowden, New York Post July 11 2019 Notre Dame Cathedral Fire went undetected for 30 minutes because of mistakes).

Update 2022

Investigators of the Notre Dame fire are only sure on one point: arson was not the cause. This declaration was made before the investigation had started. It was weeks after the fire before the investigators were finally able to safely enter the Cathedral to assess the damage and the evidence. But somehow they just knew it wasn't arson.

Now it is three years after the fire and investigators have not been able to determine the cause of the blaze at Notre Dame. Early theories involved an electrical shortage or a lit cigarette left to smolder in the construction areas above the church. These theories are improbable not only because there is no proof, but because the construction area inside the Cathedral was 45-50 feet below the attic, where the blaze started.

The latest theory is that there was an electrical shortage from the electronic bells placed near the roof. Three electronic bells were temporarily installed in the roof in 2007, along with electrical wiring. The bells rang at 18:04 on April 15, 2019, and the fire was declared at 18:20 the same evening. So there is a coincidence in timing, if nothing else.

Some newspapers have been outspoken on this point: "Electric wires were running in the roof, placed there at the express demand of the clergy. Despite the risk of short-circuiting, and in breach of all the safety regulations laid out by the chief architects of historic monuments.(see Sources for citation)"

Of course the risk of electric malfunction does not mean this caused the fire. French President Emmanuel Macron is not dwelling on causes. He is insisting the Cathedral will be repaired and open for services by 2024, which is also the year France hosts the Summer Olympics. Thus far more than 800 million francs has been donated to rebuild the Cathedral of Notre Dame.

One seriously hopes the cause of the fire was benign, not malicious. But the destruction of so much of Notre Dame Cathedral reminds Paris - and the world - of hundreds of other acts of arson and vandalism to Catholic churches in France that are not accidental. The ministry of the Interior calculates that 1,063 anti-Christian acts were committed in 2019 alone. (Frank Hawkins, What Really Caused the Notre Dame Cathedral Fire?, April 20 2020).

Church officials have consistently downplayed the anti-Catholic violence. This sort of prudence might be safer in the long run than inflaming passions (no pun intended) with conspiracy theories. One wonders, however, how much longer passions will remain restrained, and how much longer churches will be the prime targets of vandals and arsonists.

Author's note:

Music albums often have what is called a "title track." This is when one of the songs on the album is also the name of the album. It is seen as a sum up of the essence of the album: what the words and music and musicians stand for.

Tales of the Human Spirit also has a 'title track.' You have just read it. All the best of humanity and the human spirit was on display not only during the fire at Cathedral de Notre Dame, but in the previous centuries of human effort and inspiration that resulted in the creation of such an amazing edifice as the Cathedral of Notre Dame. Truly a tale of the human spirit.

Sources

Emily Bowden, New York Post July 11 2019 "Notre Dame Cathedral Fire went undetected for 30 minutes because of mistakes."

https://www.ibtimes.com/notre-dame-cathedral-fire-not-arson-875-french-churches-vandalized-2018-2785886

https://strangesounds.org/2019/07/notre-dame-fire-collapse-save-paris.html).

https://www.nytimes.com/2019/04/15/world/europe/crown-of-thorns-notre-dame.html%20?action=click&module=inline&pgtype=Article

Notre-Dame Fire Investigators Focus on Short-Circuit and Cigarettes, *New York Times,* 2019.

https://www.ibtimes.com/notre-dame-cathedral-fire-not-arson-875-french-churches-vandalized-2018-2785886

https://www.connexionfrance.com/article/French-news/Notre-Dame-fire-New-cause-investigated-as-2024-service-date-confirmed-on-second-anniversary-of-fire, by Hannah Thompson

TALES IN HARD TIMES

Antifa And The KKK

ANTIFA IS AN organization made up primarily of young white males who wear masks to hide their identity. Then they attack people without provocation or warning if those people are deemed by Antifa to be racist, a Nazi, or a white supremacist.

Antifa members decide which people are to be attacked, pepper sprayed, kicked, hit with bats, doused with liquid cement, or given brain damage. There is no vote, no debate, no proof their victims are really dastardly Nazis. In fact, Antifa victims look more normal than the LARPing Antifas do (LARP: Live Action Role Playing).

Antifa is the antithesis of democracy, and of the American belief that you are innocent until proven guilty. Antifa are un-American and un-democratic. It is an interesting irony that Antifa - a word meaning anti-fascist – uses fascist tactics. They are the very enemy they claim to be against. Even the liberal Department of Homeland Security has labeled Antifa "domestic terrorists."

Tim Pool is a left of center journalist who reports on current events in American politics and culture on several YouTube channels. He is a career journalist who has won awards for his work.

Pool recently co-hosted an event called "Ending Racism, Violence, and Totalitarianism." Guest speakers were people from all races and all points of view: liberals, moderates, progressives, traditionalists, Trumpsters, "Ultra MAGAS," and so on.

The point of the event was to talk out political differences with your political "enemies" face to face. The premise was that if you sat across the table from your political enemy and realized they were living, breathing, human beings who had things in common with you - a shared humanity, the same sports teams to root for, parenthood, the same medical problems, careers or even a shared existential angst - you would stop shouting about them and might even get along with them. So how did things go?

According to reports from people who were there, the event was a success. No, it did not permanently end racism. But yes, political opponents got to see each other's humanity, and found they had some basic commonality with their alleged enemies. Given today's climate that is a heartwarming success story - a precious step in the right direction.

The keynote speaker was Daryl Davis. Davis is a remarkable man. He is a musician and a peacekeeper. In his travels across the country playing boogie woogie piano music, he has also come to know members of the KKK - natural enemies of Davis, who is black. So, it is amazing that after getting to know Davis as a human being, 200 Klansman have turned in their robes. Yes, for real.

Daryl Davis has quietly and methodically shared his humanity with people who would like to kill him, or at least wish bad things to befall him. And he has changed their minds. His work earned him the right to be the keynote speaker for the "Ending Racism" event. After his talk he received a standing ovation from all present.

Issues of racism and free speech used to be staple issues of the Left. They still are - sort of. But now there is a "new Left" - a "regressive, authoritarian Left" according to Pool and others - who have expanded the definition of racism to include everyone except the new Left. These folks are also known as the "woke" Left because they believe they have woken up to the truth about America (here's a hint: the truth is that America is the worst country in the world - always has been, always will be). This exclusive group of woke lefties is small, but it does include Antifa.

Like the woke Left, Antifa does not support the American ideal of free speech. It supports only the speech it approves of, and nothing else. Anyone straying outside Antifa's extremely narrow world view is called names, insulted, punched, pepper sprayed, and assaulted. Small businesses have been terrorized, vandalized, and burned to the ground.

This reign of terror has always been called fascism. It is *still* fascism, even when the fascists disguise themselves with masks and with straight faces call themselves "anti-fascist." No matter what these young white males call themselves, their behavior speaks for itself.

The "anti-fascist" fascists of Antifa had their terror tactics right up front when they tried to shut down the anti-racism conference. They harassed the owners of the building holding the conference, and threatened to burn their building down. Obviously Antifa was trying to stifle speech. But why would Antifa oppose an anti-racism conference?

Well, according to Antifa, the anti-racism conference really wasn't anti-racist. It was – you guessed it - fascist. Why was it fascist? Because there were certain people attending the conference Antifa didn't like. Tim Pool for one. Pool is a self described liberal who has always voted Democrat and firmly believes in free speech. He is a publicly outspoken critic of Antifa. Another one for the Antifa enemy list is Andy Ngo, a gay Asian journalist whose work has appeared in mainstream publications like the Wall Street Journal.

Ngo was assaulted by Antifa in Portland, Oregon, during a demonstration there. Ngo was filming the event when members of Antifa surrounded him and then assaulted him from all sides. Ngo ended up with permanent brain damage as a result.

Get the picture? Anyone who disagrees with Antifa - that is, the vast majority of people - is either a fascist, a nazi, racist, or all three. The label justifies Antifa assaulting the labeled without provocation. This is how Antifa rolls. And they have the support of many in the Left, including the mainstream media, who downplay Antifa's violence and present them as mainstream. At the extreme end of discussion is President Biden's claim Antifa doesn't even exist.

But to escape the ridiculousness of that last opinion, let's settle for the mainstream media's assertion that Antifa is mainstream. This means it is mainstream behavior for Antifa to threaten to burn down buildings to prevent a conference on anti-racism. Sure, everyone does that, right?

Well, the threat worked, at least with the original promoters of the event. Allowing Antifa to bully them, the owners of the building backed down and refused to hold the event. But Pool and his co-hosts refused to be intimidated. They found another venue nearby and held their event on ending racism, violence, and totalitarianism: an agenda that would end Antifa.

Like the bullies they are, Antifa backed down when their targets refused to be intimidated. There were no attempts at arson. They did picket and demonstrate outside the event – which is certainly their right. But they could not prevent the conference from happening because their potential victims refused to be victimized.

The conference succeeded in its goals of having political

opponents talk to each other face to face. This humanized everyone. There were no keyboard warriors, no computers, phones, or other indirect forms of communication. Just face to face: conservative, progressive, moderates, everyone in one room talking to each other as one human being to another.

There were no fights, no violence, just honest communication over differences in opinion. Perhaps the majority of those in attendance left with the opinions they came in with. But they left with something more: the memory of a human being who disagreed with them, but still treated them with the respect one human deserves from another.

Daryl Davis talked about how as a black man he would communicate with KKK members as individuals. He said that over the years he influenced hundreds of KKK members to turn in their robes. "How can you hate me when you don't even know me?" he would ask them. Something in his humanity reached his political enemies.

So, the event was a success. After the conference everyone relaxed and had drinks together. Daryl Davis invited the protesting Antifa members to join the conference. It was a generous, surprising offer in a way, but it was consistent with the conference founder's belief in free speech. Free speech extends to Antifa as well.

And what better opening for Antifa to expose the anti-racism conference as the covert, clandestine fascist rally they claimed it was? Surprisingly, Antifa refused the offer to join the event. Why would they refuse an opportunity to prove the anti-racists weren't really anti-racists, that the free speech proponents really didn't support free speech?

Antifa's excuse for not joining the conference was: the conference attendees were all "white supremacists," and apparently beyond redemption. White supremacists. Really? Andy Ngo, an Asian journalist, and Daryl Davis, an African

American, were both white supremacists according to the Antifa mob. Tim Pool is a Korean American. There were more mixed race attendees at the anti-racism conference than the mostly all white Antifa crowd. You can't make this stuff up. Later Davis said that on his flight back home he kept laughing about his new moniker: white supremacist.

You do have to laugh about life sometimes. And this is one of those times. The people who really need help nowadays is Antifa. They are so confused, so angry, so screwed up politically, emotionally, and psychiatrically that you do have to feel for them.

They seem to realize they would be exposed as hollow shells if they ever tried to verbally debate issues. That is the reason Antifa did not accept the invitation to join the conference. If some compassionate people could just sit down and talk with them, what would happen? Perhaps they would turn in their masks, just as the KKK members turned in their robes.

Because when it comes down to it, Antifa and the KKK are two sides of the same coin. The only difference is that Antifa hasn't been shut down like the KKK. For the welfare and humanity of suffering Antifas everywhere, let us hope that difference is just a matter of time.

Author's Note

There is evidence Antifa worked with the FBI in a false flag operation during the January 6 protests at the nation's capital. Antifa was there, punching people (yawn) and calling everyone fascists. Many Antifas got punched back, then retreated when a show of force appeared to oppose them.

It is claimed at least one Antifa agent was walking around with blood on his face. He was claiming the police beat him, and seemed to be trying to incite the protesters to violence.

It turns out his "blood" was stage blood you can buy at a magic and costume store. He was confronted about this and slipped away into the crowd. So is Antifa working with our government now? Is our government really working with what it calls domestic terrorists? Hmmm...

(See https://www.theepochtimes.com/luke-coffee-says-god-told-him-to-stand-in-the-gap-on-january-6_4492954.html?)

Couldn't Stand
The Weather

STEVIE RAY VAUGHAN'S break out song was "Couldn't Stand The Weather." It was the title track to his album which was also a best seller. Although he left us way too early (age 35 in a helicopter crash), Stevie Ray had his share of natural disasters growing up in Texas.

Maybe some of the following acts of nature inspired Vaughan's song: wildfires, floods, hurricanes, severe storms, tornadoes, extreme heat, landslides, and power outages. Through no fault of his own, however, Stevie Ray never had to face a snow blizzard.

It's easy to live dangerously in the land of 10,000 snowstorms. Stay here a few winters in Minnesota and you will understand. Yesterday I drove to work on unplowed freeways. I could see fifty feet ahead of me before everything turned white. The trick in white out conditions is to stay on the road, no matter how slow you have to go. A maniac roared by me, lost control, spun his car in a complete circle and disappeared into the white. I kept crawling forward and made it to work in one piece.

Smarter employees wouldn't have risked their necks for the nickel. I found this out when I got to work and realized how short staffed we were. Then there was the small matter of getting out of the parking lot at the end of the work night. The entrance was plugged by two feet of plowed, compacted snow. The parking lot had a foot of snow, and a nasty incline that had me spinning my tires trying to get out. At 12:30 am I began shoveling the parking lot. One hour later my co-workers came outside to check my vital signs.asked

I was okay. Fortunately I had given up cigars fifty days ago. This allowed me to shovel, and shovel, and shovel. And spin, and spin, and spin my tires. I had meant to get new tires during the last snowstorm, but a week of balmy weather lulled my tightwad self into a false sense of security. A patient came out and asked: "Do you need a push?" Then he warned: "I don't want to hurt myself." "Just give me some moral support," I told him.

I backed up once more, then approached the incline in first gear, driving very slowly to keep my tires from spinning. I inched up the incline, and made it through the narrow opening I had shoveled at the end of the parking lot. I slipped through to the safety of a plowed road that eventually led me home.

The trip home was a journey surreal: lots of deserted, snow-covered freeways punctuated by the flashing lights of cars in ditches. As I neared home a tow truck and highway patrol car assisted a stuck Humvee. Thunder and lightning accompanied the falling snow. No, I'm not kidding.

I got home around 2 am , and shoveled my sidewalks so the city wouldn't ticket me. This morning I shoveled my vehicle out again after it became trapped in snow from the city plows coming down the alley. It is still snowing, and I will have more shoveling tonight, and probably tomorrow. But for now I am warm. My belly is full and I will abide.

Some people move when they can't stand the weather. There is nothing wrong with that, of course, but bad weather has a way of catching up with everyone; no matter what we do to try to avoid it. Call it character building. Call it God's way of getting even with us; or if you are pious, call it God's way of drawing us closer to himself.

I haven't been pious for a while. Hypocrite that I am, however, I prayed for safe journeys through the blizzards. Who knows? Maybe the Catholic patient who came to check on me also said a prayer for me. Maybe his prayer for me was heard while mine went into the recycling bin. But I did make it home; maybe I had some help.

One day all the questions will be answered; this is what believers believe anyway. For now, it doesn't matter if you can't stand the weather. All you have to do is figure out a way to live through it.

A Winter's Tale

THE FUNERAL HOME was impressive from the outside. But the dignity of the white pillars standing guard outside the large double doors disappeared when you stepped inside and walked on old carpeting into a dimly lit room with dark wood paneling.

Across the room were a pair of lime green armchairs embossed with tarnished silver studs. One of the chairs held an old guy - probably the custodian. He was up for some company and I wasn't in a hurry. He brought out hot, strong coffee. I gulped it down, hoping the heat would raise my body temperature.

Up in northern Minnesota, he told me, they bury the dead in vaults above the ground during winter. Down here in tropical St. Paul, however, everyone goes underground. "Backhoes, power hammers, whatever it takes," he said cheerfully, explaining that after the machines pierced the frost line, winter grave digging offered no special challenges.

"Are you the pastor?" he asked, nodding at the thick black book I held in the hand that wasn't holding the coffee. I shook my head: "I was his social worker." He nodded again. "Nice of you to come."

He handed me an annual calendar card that, right under the funeral chapel's name and the American flag, listed him as the director. We talked a while longer, then he excused himself. He came back and said "They're out there in the new cemetery. You'll want to drive your car. Just park it behind the hearse. Take your coffee with you. They're probably waiting for you."

The wind hurled snow at my face as I hurried to my car. It started, and I took off, not bothering to turn on the heater because it was one of those days where you just never get warm. I parked behind the white hearse, swallowed more coffee, and joined the huddled group of three men: the undertaker, his assistant, and an acquaintance of the dead man. The looks they gave me made it clear. They *had* been waiting for me, standing in the cold.

We introduced ourselves and made small talk while the wind burned our cheeks and our toes went numb. The undertaker's assistant pointed behind us to some frozen flower bouquets sticking out of a mound of snow. "Did that one yesterday," he said. "A 14 year old boy." Car accident? I asked. "Nah," he said. "He went into the hospital three years ago for surgery and came out a vegetable. Couldn't talk or nothing. A damn shame. It's a real blessing he died."

We turned away from the wind to our coffin. It rested on two thick straps that wound around a broad stainless steel frame. At the proper time, the contraption would mechanically lower the coffin into the ground. Behind the grave a chain link fence separated the cemetery from Interstate Highway 96. Sometimes we felt a shudder from the impact of air being displaced by speeding cars.

The undertaker asked if I wanted to say some prayers. He deferred to me, I suspected, because the county I worked for was paying for the funeral, and he was unsure if I was attending as a mourner or to make sure county money was being well spent. Yes, I said, I would say some prayers.

I opened the Saint Andrew's Missal, made the sign of

the cross and read Psalm 129, the *De Profundis*, in English. We were about 30 feet from the highway and I found my voice rising to compete with passing trucks and cars. Then a plane flew overhead, drowning out the plea: "Out of the depths I have cried to Thee, O Lord! Lord hear my voice."

Next I read in the Burial Mass, ending awkwardly, it felt, with the prayer for absolution. A priest should be doing this, not me. But this was a county burial, not a funeral; besides, we weren't even sure the dead man had ever been baptized.

Part of the problem was that the dead man, when alive, often gave conflicting information about himself. I wasn't even sure his real name was Charles, although he answered to it. Different people got different versions about when Charles' birthday was, what his Social Security number was, which war he was in, whether or not he was married, whether or not he had children, and so on. I don't think Charles was trying to confuse people; I think *he* was confused about things.

Years of drinking had given Charles what we indelicately call 'a wet brain': the symptoms resembled dementia. Charles and his muddled memory were staying at a homeless shelter until he started heaving up blood. At the hospital they discovered he had lung cancer. The surgeon took out half a lung, then sent Charles to a nursing home to recuperate from surgery.

Charles recovered so completely that he started assaulting people. He was taken to the psych ward and some genius diagnosed him as mentally ill. I was told to find him another place to live.

The last year of Charles' life was spent in a different nursing home. Charles stopped fighting, but turned to stealing cigarettes and staying out past curfew. He developed prostate cancer. Then his kidneys started failing. Charles became too weak to panhandle on University Avenue. For his own safety he was placed on the locked unit of the nursing home. Like a caged bird, he wilted. The last time I talked to him he recognized me but was too weak and confused to say much. I didn't tell him things would be okay however, because he wasn't *that* confused.

There is no remedy for renal failure, but Charles rallied briefly anyway. He even ate solid food for a few days;. On Sunday night staff checked his vital signs. All was well. Charles fell asleep and a few hours later died quietly, alone in his bed.

The home destroyed all of Charles' clothes. They were so thorough that Charles had no burial clothes. Not that it mattered. His was a closed casket funeral without family, friends, or coworkers. There weren't even any enemies. Charles left this world in a winding cloth and nothing else.

The acquaintance at Charles' burial was a retired bus driver named Bruce. He had talked to Charles a couple of times while visiting Charles' roommate at the nursing home. After the prayers at Charles' grave Bruce sang a verse of a Swedish hymn in a clear, strong tenor voice. Then Bruce told me of a night Charles said, "I know I'm dying and I want to get right with God."

Bruce said, "I sat with Charles and we prayed together, and he accepted Jesus as his personal savior." After a moment Bruce said "It was the kind of meeting I dream about."

We watched the coffin drop into the dark hole, smoothly and quietly. Traffic continued to zoom by. The undertaker shook our hands and left, leaving it to his assistant to complete the burial. Bruce made a joke about his mother calling *De Profundis* the "scuba divers prayer." I stared at him. Then, for some reason, I told Bruce I had prevented Charles from being cremated. He shook his head in irritation. "It doesn't matter what happens to our bodies. We are spirit. When we rise again we get glorified bodies. The Bible says 'the sea will give up its dead.'"

I wasn't sure how all those thoughts were connected to each other. I thought about explaining the anti-Christian origins of cremation, how the cremation societies of the 19th century were masonic in origin; their motives were to emphasize materialism and de-emphasize the religious dogma of the resurrection of the body.

Instead I tried a more familiar response, remarking that St. Paul said our bodies were temples of the Holy Spirit. "Yes, if you possess the Holy Spirit," Bruce said with a glint in his eye. Fair enough, I thought. I looked Bruce square in the eye, shook his hand and smiled: "One day we'll know for sure." Then we parted.

Charles was not only materially unencumbered when he left this world. His sole spiritual sustenance was meager too: the best wishes of a Protestant passerby and the hope against hope prayers of his Catholic social worker for Charles' soul. It was oddly fitting that Charles died on December 10: the feast of Our Lady of Loreto. Loreto, Italy is the site of the Holy House of Nazareth, said to have been transported from Nazareth to Loreto by angels. Maybe the prayers for Charles, so frequently homeless, persuaded Our Lady to bring Charles to his real home.

Yes, it's a long shot - a real long shot. But to deny the possibility of prayer changing a soul's destination is not to be Catholic or Christian. Besides, winter has set in, and it's already tough enough to feel warm.

Requiem For Tommy

I REMEMBER TOMMY very well. Tommy's not his real name, we don't identify people in my business - and that is a good thing.

Tommy was six feet seven inches tall and weighed 260 pounds. A huge man with very little fat on his bones. A ferocious football player who, it is said, pulled an iron seclusion door off its hinges at a state hospital. I don't believe this, but if anyone could have done that -it would have been Tommy.

So you didn't want to mess with Tommy. Especially when he wasn't taking the Lithium capsules that kept him from staying up all night and being a large menace to anyone crossing his path.

When Tommy took his medications he felt depressed. When he didn't take the medications he got very happy. Tommy liked the power, the "Vrooom" rush of energy from the mania of his bipolar disorder. Once he led the police on a twenty-mile car chase, doing 100 mph and more the whole way. Wasn't much left of his car when it was finished, but Tommy was feeling fine - fine enough to give a half dozen officers a very hard time.

I was part of a county mental health team working with Tommy. We respected each other but we had our clashes. I remember him looking down at me a few times with murder in his eyes. I knew he wanted to take me out, and he certainly could have, but he never did.

Tommy was a born again fella and liked to talk about his religion. Once he showed me a thirty-page paper he had written about the end times. I told him: if you ever want to get serious about religion you'll have to turn Catholic. He laughed and shook his head.

I transferred to another county and lost touch with Tommy. A few years later I read in the paper he took a dive off the High Bridge over the Mississippi River in St. Paul. The high bridge is where the seriously suicidal people go. Few people leave the bridge and survive. Tommy was no exception - he didn't make it to shore alive.

I always figured Tommy would go out taking people with him – didn't take him for a suicide. But he was sick for a long time, and the sickness takes its toll on the brain, which made his life even harder. Guess it got too hard for Tommy, and he made his own end times.

A lot of people die in my line of work. Clients and co-workers. I stopped counting a few years ago when it was over two dozen. Its a damn hard world to start with, and being sick can make things well-nigh unbearable. One poor gal I knew immolated herself and survived in acute agony for a couple of months before the end came. There is no lack of suffering in this world; the survivors come to terms with it. I don't judge those who don't. I pray for them.

Requiescat in pacem

Broken Home Boys

IN MY NECK of the woods the Catholic contribution to the liberal welfare state is the Dorothy Day Center (DDC), a long, one-story brick affair skulking in the shadow of the St. Paul Cathedral.

Straddling the I-94 freeway and the Greyhound Bus Depot, the DDC is a convenient location for the largest concentration of pure characters in the Twin Cities of St. Paul and Minneapolis: vagrants, drunks, addicts, criminals, professional hobos, the mentally ill, and more of the same just arriving on their one way bus tickets from Chicago and Gary, Indiana.

In addition to being a hub for underground commerce (that is, drug deals), the DDC offers "three hots and a cot" - meals and a mat to sleep on in the winter - to all comers. That's where Carlton was hanging out until he started carving tattoos into his forearms, talking about slitting people's throats, and following female staff when they left work. Social justice Catholics help the homeless until things get ugly, then they turn people like Carlton over to people like me.

The deal was that Carlton would go voluntarily to the local psych ward if I helped him pick up his clothes first. I didn't trust it, but I wasn't the one who made the deal - the DDC folks rolled Carlton at me like a big, bad penny. I remember our receptionist's grateful look when I hustled him out of our lobby onto the street. He loped along next to me, a secret smile on his face. I'd seen that look before. It happens when the voices get more real than reality.

In my car he pointed at a little statue on the dashboard - "that's Momma Mary." We got to his friend's house, a weathered duplex on the North Side of St. Paul. Carlton went inside the front door, and out through the back. After waiting a few minutes I knew Carlton had given me the slip, but I stayed until I'd finished praying for him, and the others.

I knew I'd see Carlton again, and when he ended up in the psych ward I paid him a visit. I reminded him of how he scammed me. He laughed and apologized. I smiled back and told him I was arranging a vacation for him at the state hospital. Usually this bothers people, but Carlton liked the hospital. He'd stayed at worse places, like the Southern prison he never wanted to talk about.

In my line of work we are expected to fix people. Sometimes we can. Other times its like mending spokes on a broken wheel that never rolls straight. Carlton was one of the broken wheels.

He came from a broken family and it became a habit. He kept breaking every chance he had at keeping a roof over his head. Three group home placements failed because Carlton couldn't play by the rules, at least not for long. Eventually he'd start doing drugs. Then he'd steal from and bully his peers to get money to do more drugs.

Finally I sent him out of town to a cabin in the north western Minnesota woods. Carlton didn't like all the trees, or the way things got so quiet at night. After he was caught trying to steal a van he barricaded himself in the medication office. The local sheriff extricated him. They brought Carlton back to St. Paul, in shackles, and dropped him off at the emergency room at St. Joseph's Hospital. Once more he broke the rules of the commitment order a judge placed on him. His commitment was revoked. Out of options, I sent him back to the state hospital.

Eventually I found another group home who would take Carlton. They got him his own apartment and helped him move in. Someone came over every night to watch him take the medication that dulled the voices in his head. I'd come over once a month to buy groceries for him and tell him to quit doing drugs with the home boys.

The last time I saw Carlton alive I threatened him with another trip to the state hospital if he didn't straighten out. Carlton got mad, then asked me for a ride home. On the way to his place Carlton warned me we were driving through a bad part of town. "There's a lot of blacks around here," he said nervously. It was a curious remark, since Carlton was black.

Two days later Carlton was at a friend's apartment. The friend stuck a knife in Carlton's chest because he didn't like the way Carlton was whispering to the voices under his breath. Later the friend said he was surprised Carlton didn't stab him back. According to him, Carlton pulled the knife out of his chest, told his friend he didn't want to hurt him, and ran out the door with the knife. The police followed the blood in the snow to a nearby house. It was there that the blood, and Carlton's life, stopped.

The funeral was at a local Baptist church. It might have been a Catholic church once. There were a few panes of stained glass, wings off the main church where side altars used to be, and tall dark paneling where confessionals once stood. A table replaced the altar and a choir replaced the tabernacle. Everyone who spoke at the open microphone was convinced Carlton was in heaven. Reasons for this location were not given.

A somber, dignified minister seemed to think otherwise,

but limited his remarks to noting that Carlton died well, and that, no, the black community was not going to make an issue out of Carlton's assailant being white. Violent death had changed Carlton's appearance, and I found myself looking at a man I barely recognized. Perhaps the most useful thing I ever did for Carlton happened at the funeral. I prayed for his soul.

Its a bad sign when people you know end up on the front page because of the way they died. It happened with Carlton, and then with Gina. I'd worked with her for awhile in another county. She was a product of Catholic high school, but she had to ask me the words to the Hail Mary prayer. I told her, and encouraged her to visit the Blessed Sacrament at a church near our office between client appointments.

Gina was sincerely religious, but she'd fallen away from the Church after her parents divorced. Fervent in everything she did, she became a fervent Protestant who occasionally attended Mass at a charismatic Catholic church. Yet she kept some Catholic instincts, and lived virtuously. Maybe I imagined it, but she seemed to be turning towards a real faith when we parted ways. She came to mind from time to time as someone to pray for.

The last time I saw her alive she was excited about her upcoming marriage. Glenn was a Protestant, she said, and they were "negotiating" their religious beliefs. More than anything else Gina wanted to get married and have a family, so she ended up negotiating away her Catholicism. She married and a year later gave birth to a baby girl, Amanda.

The baby had health problems the doctors could not fix. Gina's distress grew when Amanda started having seizures medication could not stop. She started talking about killing her daughter so she (the baby) wouldn't have to suffer anymore. Apparently no one took her seriously, including perhaps Gina herself.

Little Amanda died. Two days later Gina stole a handgun and rented a hotel room. She called Glenn and confessed to smothering their daughter with a pillow. Then she said she was going to kill herself. Glenn and Gina's family called all hotels in town. They didn't find Gina's hotel until the end of the day. By then it was too late to do anything but arrange a double funeral.

It was held at a strip mall in a renovated space that used to be a supermarket my mother shopped at when I was growing up. There was nothing outside the main entrance that identified it as a church, just a street number. The inside was dark. The carpet was dark. The walls were dark. There were no religious symbols, not even a cross. In front there was a large stage, and a huge black curtain. Next to the stage was a small coffin and a larger one. Both were open. Amanda looked like she was sleeping. Gina just looked dead.

Glenn stood in the back, behind the dozens of perfectly rowed chairs of black plastic and gleaming metal. He stared at the front of the room where his family lay in boxes. I went over to him. I tried to explain who I was and realized it didn't matter. I groped, and then said, "It was to your credit that she loved you." He turned his eyes from the stage onto me. Tears streamed silently down his face. I mumbled something well meaning and stupid, and left him alone.

The middle of the church was filled with sound equipment. To the left was a raised platform where an expensive looking video camera rested on a tripod. The technical crew bounced back and forth between the two stations, checking sound and lighting. A soundtrack was playing a Natalie Merchant song. The chorus repeated "Thank you, thank you, I want to thank you." It was intended as a tribute to Gina, who had many friends. As one of her friends I had a savage impulse to destroy both the song and the equipment that played it.

The clarity of the music was remarkable, however. Probably the video was of high quality too. The funeral service was called a celebration of Gina's life. A few of her friends came up to the microphone and spoke well of her. They were all convinced she was in heaven with her baby and her Lord. I made to leave. Then one of the pastors got up and finally admitted that some people were angry at Gina, and worried about where she might be. I stopped at the back and listened.

You have permission to be angry, the pastor said, but he urged us to move beyond that. As for where Gina was, well, he too was convinced she was in heaven because Gina had personally accepted Jesus as her Savior. Never underestimate God's love, he told us. Would an infinitely loving God forsake one of his beloved children on a technicality? Impossible. I had never before heard a double murder called a technicality.

It was time to go, but I stopped in the lobby to look at several easels of pictures of Glenn, Gina, and their baby. They looked happy and content, smiling right into the camera. Glenn's eyes were mild and kind. I wondered how long it would be before he looked that way again.

Carlton and Glenn had little in common. One was a ne'er do well with no permanent address for most of his life. The other was a young lawyer with a big house, a beautiful wife and the start of a family. What they shared was broken homes. Carlton broke all of his, and Glenn's home was broken by Gina.

In a larger sense, however, both men were broken off from their eternal home. For if God is the ultimate reality, he was absent from both funerals I attended, lacking as they did any sense of reality. Is God really just an infinite, look-the-other way pillow that embraces everyone no matter what they have done in their lives? If he is, then does it really matter how we conduct ourselves here below? Heaven is an amoral elevator repeatedly dinging its way to the top floor. All you have to do is be patient and wait your turn.

Most of us sense things don't really work that way. Consequently, a religion that shrugs off murder as a technicality, or ignores it altogether, just doesn't make sense. Such a religion has no justice, no standards of conduct, and provides no real reason to consider your life, or how you live it, as having any significance. I could understand someone going to either funeral I attended and leaving with a feeling of contempt for a God who didn't seem to stand for anything except love and hugs.

May God rest her tortured soul, I don't think Gina believed in a marshmallow God either. I don't pretend to know why she did what she did, but I guess she couldn't endure her baby's suffering, or persevere under the strain of helplessly witnessing it. She had always wanted a family, but what we want from life is often quite different once we finally get it. Even so, murder and suicide were the last things I would have expected from an outspoken pro-lifer like Gina.

Perhaps post-partum depression, or something worse, affected her thinking. That doesn't excuse what she did, but it may be a partial explanation. After she smothered her baby she realized the enormity of her deed. If her former clarity concerning right and wrong returned, this may have caused her to despair. Or perhaps the clarity led her to pass sentence, and execute judgment upon herself.

I like to think that if Gina had returned to a real faith this would have averted the insanity of her final days.

Is that too easy an answer? Perhaps, but its clear that whatever religion she was practicing dissolved when it was needed the most. Ask her widowed husband, who is left to seek solace where he can find it. Solace will be as elusive as justice, if he remains true to the platitudes of his non-denominational warehouse religion.

My old *confrere* Carlton had five uncles and cousins who became Baptist ministers, but he was more intent on finding solace in drugs than his family's religion. It was a deadly mistake, but maybe he thought he already knew enough about religion to not take it seriously. Or perhaps, when he realized he couldn't take religion seriously, he gave up.

If that's what happened, I know a lot of guys like Carlton. When times get tough, we look for the real religion. When we only get lies or half-truths we don't doubt only the liars; we may begin to doubt our God-given instinct to search for our Creator. Anger can result. We may decide we hate God but what we really hate is being unable to find him, and having to put up with liars.

True religion provides ultimate truth. Truth is hard like life, but the hardness of truth is another word for justice, which provides its own solace, and an eternal lifeline for Carlton, for Glenn, and for all the broken home boys.

Lullaby For Ricky

ONE OF RICKY'S earliest memories was doing drugs with his family. One day a prostitute came over to babysit and injected heroin between Ricky's toes. He never forgot the pain, or the high that pulsed through his body like waves until exhausted, he nodded off and fell asleep in his crib.

With drugs came violence to which Ricky was witness and victim. Perhaps he was present when his mother attempted suicide. Perhaps he was there when his father, stoned to his gills, kidnapped a woman and had an armed standoff with the Minneapolis police. Small surprise that Ricky got a pellet gun for his birthday. He dropped piles of bird seed in the backyard and waited. Ricky was a good shot; soon there were bird corpses all over the yard.

While other boys were building tree houses, Ricky built a miniature gas chamber and fashioned small, impeccably tied nooses. Ricky dissected living animals, removing eyes, skin, and organs from neighborhood pets. It was this behavior that first brought Ricky to the attention of law enforcement. He would learn to like being locked up - it offered a structure and sense of predictability Ricky's home life could not duplicate. At least in prison Ricky's mom couldn't steal the pills Ricky's psychiatrist gave him.

He grew up bouncing between chemical dependency treatment and prison. Ricky regretted his tormenting of animals, and developed a talent for manual labor. His favorite job was cleaning skyscraper windows. He made a trade out of it - when he wasn't doing time for drugs or assault.

Ricky had a mean streak that surfaced when he ran out of drugs. When he told his probation officer that he would tie her up, make her watch Ricky kill her husband, then rape her and cut her up into little pieces he probably meant it. He had a rep as a badass and had messed other people up. After doing a *lot* of extra time for shooting his mouth off to his PO, Ricky learned to keep terroristic thoughts to himself. He kept his hands busy fashioning hangman's nooses of all shapes and sizes out of ropes, cords, even sewing thread.

Ricky never had much chance of a normal life. When he suppressed his violence it turned inward, causing depression and thoughts of suicide. Ricky overdosed on heroin a lot but survived each one; he wasn't trying to kill himself, he told me; he just wanted to get higher, to feel better.

He crushed pain medications and injected them into his body, and survived this too. But he had a lot of other overdose attempts he couldn't shrug off as failed highs. By this point in his life the only crimes Ricky was committing were against himself. He went from the criminal system to the mental health system. "If you let me out I will kill myself," he told his doctor at the state hospital. Tough luck Ricky, no one gets to stay in state hospitals indefinitely anymore. It was decided Ricky needed ECT - electro convulsive therapy, commonly known as shock treatments.

ECT is a last resort treatment used to treat intractable symptoms of paranoia and depression. It works but carries a price tag: you lose your memory and your personality - yet at least you are alive and not thinking of killing yourself all the time. After months of ECT treatments the state hospital wanted to discharge him to my facility. I remember interviewing Ricky. He was a muscular, tattooed 30 year old with long sandy blond hair. He looked me in the eye and said he wanted to get better. I don't know what hit me harder: his sincerity or his pain. We decided to give Ricky a chance.

Ricky had sworn off heroin, which was a good thing. He replaced it with K-2, which was a bad thing. At the time K-2 was legal in Minnesota. It was sold in tobacco stores and head shops as incense. K-2 does contain incense, and a lot of other processed materials that are not good for your body or your mind, including a powerful, synthetic form of cannabis that not only gives you a righteous high, it makes you see things too.

Ricky was still receiving ECT treatments even though he was not in the state hospital anymore. The combination of ECT and K-2 fried Ricky's brain so badly he couldn't remember his name. The last time I saw Ricky I was helping him put his bags in the back of the sheriff's van that had come to take him back to the state hospital. We shook hands. I'll never forget the look in his eyes. I didn't see sincerity, or even pain. I saw total confusion. We hadn't helped Ricky at all.

Later I heard Ricky was discharged from the state hospital and was doing okay living down south. For addicts, success can be as deadly as failure. Both make you want to use. Ricky got a hold of some smack. He hadn't shot up in years. The smack was too pure for Ricky's system, and he took too much. Years before he could have done the same amount of H - or more - without incident. This time the heroin killed him.

I remembered all the failed overdose attempts Ricky made. Isn't it life that the time he didn't want to overdose he killed himself? It is remarkable Ricky lived so long. What child imbibing heroin with his mother's milk has any chance in life? Like ducks who walk after the first moving object they see and call it mama, Ricky's mama was heroin.

Even when Ricky and mama weren't talking, mama was always waiting around the corner, waiting for her boy to come back, to hold him in her arms, to stroke his long, blond hair, and to whisper in his ear:

Lullabye life, lullabye death; lullaby smack and lullabye meth; my sweet baby boy let me bleed you white so you die in my arms and sleep the sleep of the lost where Hades and Heaven are the same white light, as pure as the rush of my poison in your little boy veins.

And from a former friend who couldn't help you Ricky, but can still say: Hush-a-bye little boy, hush-a-bye man of crimes, may God show you the mercy you never had, the mercy you never learned to give yourself. And if God has no mercy for you let him be no God of mine.

Chamber Music

THE FALL RAINS come as the leaves are dying. The drops paint the leaves, splashing on shades of yellow, red, and gold as both fall from the sky. The wooded banks of the river turn from a uniform green to a riot of color. The panorama extends for miles but invisibly, when a bend in the river brackets the vista like the border of a picture post card.

I mark the changes on my daily drive across the Mississippi River bridge, an arced span that ends at the Ford automotive plant on the St. Paul side of the river. Like art imitating life, people begin imitating nature. They don't turn different colors, but they accelerate as if they too are under the spell of a wind that makes leaves float, spin, stop, and dance away. Like the leaves, people are looking for a place to rest.

There are lots of trees at the state hospital known as Anoka Metro Regional Treatment Center ("Anoka" for short). Like many of the patients, the leaves here seem to be resting. I knew a man who lived at the state hospital for ten years straight, which proves you can get used to just about anything. It does not mean you enjoy it. Random shouts, screams, and curses emanate from the aging brick buildings. I'm a social worker, and all my folks are in locked units.

You meet all kinds at Anoka because insanity doesn't discriminate. Rich, poor, men, women, educated and not. There are schizophrenics; bipolars; the depressed and suicidal; chronic alcoholics whose use has given them wet brains (we call it dementia now); "MI and D's" (mentally ill and dangerous); the religiously delusional; satanists; a swarm of personality disorders; assorted misfits and malingering criminals who prefer the mental health system to prison.

The commerce in this community of the unwell revolves around sex, drugs, cigarettes and pop - not necessarily in that order. There is never enough to go around. Sometimes frustration sets in and patients' prey on each other. The collective misery attracts demons like flies to a carcass. They goad and taunt the unfortunates, enhancing the general misery.

The cruel afflictions these human beings share are not soothed by the Muzak piped in through hospital speakers. The incessant group therapies are not welcome either. Neither are medications that make them drool and shuffle. But this is the result when you are unable to make it in the cold hard world.

And within each of them is a small, enclosed space - a chamber. On occasion I have entered a chamber and paused for a time in a landscape utterly different from the cool, color filled land of creation.

Some chamber terrains are bleak and silent. Others are pain filled, all a throb in reds and blacks. Here are landscapes of terror, despair, profound sadness and madness - so interwoven it is impossible to tell if madness is a cause or an effect. The writhing, inconsolable quality of some chambers echoes the silent screams of lost souls. My instincts tell me to pray and run.

I leave, but they do not always leave me. Their wretchedness is haunting. One of the few taboos remaining in our culture is insanity. Mental illness is a leprous scab that strips its bearer of all credibility and social standing. You can get away with a lot these days, but you'd better not lose your marbles - or have someone accuse you of it.

I knew of this stigma before I met the poor folk. Like the biblical "sins of the father," research says schizophrenia runs in families. It runs in mine.

By the grace of God or luck of the draw I've been spared, but not entirely. There are memory fragments from childhood that still detonate with force. I remember Dad when the voices took over. They kept him awake, told him to kill himself, told him we were all against him. He hurt himself. He hurt us. Dad bled. We bled. Our home received a mournful baptism of tears and blood.

At his peak Dad got hyper religious and violent - a nasty big man with mayhem in his eyes chasing a little boy. Me. The neighbors called the police, who cornered Dad and dragged him out of the house. Slowly the echoes of shouts, screams, and sirens died away. Our home sat shrouded in silence and shame.

Now I hospitalize people. Sometimes it feels like I'm still trying to hospitalize Dad so he can finally get the help he needed years ago. Maybe my career is an attempt to mend the damage done to our family, as if I could retroactively transform my real childhood into the childhood I needed to have. But not even lies can change the past.

Dad got better before he died. He loved my wife and kids, and they laughed when he mixed up their names. He never apologized or spoke of what his madness did to us - or what it did to him. But he tried to make amends without saying so, and sometimes I tried to let him. He was better at this than I was. It is sad I could not love him but being unable to forgive him hurt more. Gradually a will to forgive appeared like a bud on a tree. On my better days I willed that it grow.

It helped that he was kind to my children. They loved

their grandpa. They taught him how to return affection - or reminded him how he did it before his life went to hell. Then one day Dad was on his deathbed. He had failed quickly and profoundly. Life support sustained him until my sisters and I arrived.

There was no question of prolonging his life, only how we would say good-bye. I had my few minutes alone. I knew Dad could never hurt us again, and I talked to him. I didn't tell him I loved him, but I told him I forgave him, and I asked him to forgive me. I heard him sigh. We gathered at his bed. They pulled the plug and we watched Dad die.

I never tried to enter Dad's chamber. Whenever I got too close I veered away. He gave me what he had: his pain and suffering. I accepted it for what it was: a legacy. I share my legacy in an unspoken way with the folk I work with.

They give me what they have: their misery and broken-ness. They are the humblest of gifts, and I accept their gifts with respect - something that was too hard for me to do with my own father because I wanted and needed so much more from him.

The results of my work are none of my business, I sup-pose. It has been a privilege to have been able to enter the tortured chambers of my fellow humans: to pay my respects, to bear witness to their pain, and to pray for their healing. Sometimes I think they know. I hope my pres-ence makes a difference: if not with their illness, or even with their wretched lives, then at least with their spiritual welfare.

In return, I have been rewarded, perhaps excessively. For as the fall rains come to all, so has the ancient gift of tears come to me. They mingle with the rain, and I embrace everything that washes over a heart no longer hidden, a heart broken yet woken as well. I realize I am growing to love what was never there, to love all that I never had, for it has made me the man, the husband, and the father I am today. And that is a good thing.

The leaves are falling faster now. They carpet the ground, and cold mornings coat fallen leaves with frost. Some trees are almost bare, skeletal limbs anticipating the tomb of winter. The fidelity of nature's design is admirable. The organized miracle called "change of season" helps me believe it is never - ever - too late for grace. I take my children to a park. We swing and play in the leaves. The youngest ones run to me laughing. We hug. I am leaving them a legacy too. After they are in bed the house is quiet. I think about home. I close my eyes and listen, for sounds of chamber music.

Author Back Page

THANK YOU FOR reading this book. I have been writing for most of my adult life. Yet I have never tired of wrestling with words; phrases; thoughts and fragments of thought; chopping paragraphs in two; trimming run on sentences (like this one); and on and on...in short, the glorious tedium of working with words.

God invented word processors for writers, or at least for *this* writer. Without it I couldn't have written the five books and dozens of articles published over the years. That of course does not include essays and other written product produced under duress during college and law school.

College I worked my way through with a major in psychology and a minor in philosophy. Law school I also worked my way through. Then I graduated, passed the 2 day bar exam, and was admitted to practice law.

Other changes involved sobering up, converting to Catholicism, and beginning to raise a family of seven children. They are young adults now. It is with pride and relief that I see them making their way in the adult world. They have it much tougher now than I had it at their ages. Life in America has been brutal: especially these last few years when the powerful seem to delight in lying to, mocking, and squashing the common folk.

I began working with adults having legal entanglements,

mental illness, and chemical dependency. Over time I became a licensed social worker for the state of Minnesota. This career became a calling for me. Along with my new career, and my station in life as a husband and a dad to a large family, I started writing articles and then books at night - something I do to this day. Writing is also a calling for me. I don't have a choice: I have to write.

In my spare time I work out at the gym, curate music, garden, and celebrate family birthdays. My beautiful and gracious wife Nelia keeps me in line. There is a blog I have on WordPress that contains a lot of my articles (including the ones published here). It is called "True Tales Well Told," and you can find it at moina-arcee.blog. Thanks again for checking out *Tales of the Human Spirit.* Watch for my next book.

CPSIA information can be obtained
at www.ICGtesting.com
Printed in the USA
JSHW051919070822
28999JS00001B/1